Gender Equality in Chile

TOWARDS A BETTER SHARING OF PAID AND UNPAID WORK

OECD

BETTER POLICIES FOR BETTER LIVES

This work is published under the responsibility of the Secretary-General of the OECD. The opinions expressed and arguments employed herein do not necessarily reflect the official views of OECD member countries.

This document, as well as any data and map included herein, are without prejudice to the status of or sovereignty over any territory, to the delimitation of international frontiers and boundaries and to the name of any territory, city or area.

The statistical data for Israel are supplied by and under the responsibility of the relevant Israeli authorities. The use of such data by the OECD is without prejudice to the status of the Golan Heights, East Jerusalem and Israeli settlements in the West Bank under the terms of international law.

Note by Turkey

The information in this document with reference to "Cyprus" relates to the southern part of the Island. There is no single authority representing both Turkish and Greek Cypriot people on the Island. Turkey recognises the Turkish Republic of Northern Cyprus (TRNC). Until a lasting and equitable solution is found within the context of the United Nations, Turkey shall preserve its position concerning the "Cyprus issue".

Note by all the European Union Member States of the OECD and the European Union

The Republic of Cyprus is recognised by all members of the United Nations with the exception of Turkey. The information in this document relates to the area under the effective control of the Government of the Republic of Cyprus.

Please cite this publication as:
OECD (2021), *Gender Equality in Chile: Towards a Better Sharing of Paid and Unpaid Work*, OECD Publishing, Paris, *https://doi.org/10.1787/6cc8ea3e-en*.

ISBN 978-92-64-81328-1 (print)
ISBN 978-92-64-56126-7 (pdf)

Foreword

The OECD review of *Gender Equality in Chile* is the first in a series addressing Latin American and Caribbean countries on this particular topic. It puts gender gaps in labour and educational outcomes in Chile into a comparative context, elaborating on the factors that contribute to unequal outcomes, including the uneven distribution of unpaid work. It investigates how existing policies and programmes in Chile can contribute to making this distribution more equitable, providing suggestions on how to strengthen them.

Closing gender gaps in paid and unpaid work responsibilities is not only a moral and social imperative but also a central part of any successful strategy for stronger, more sustainable and more inclusive growth. The COVID-19 crisis and the associated lock-down measures have placed this cause at the top of the agenda of all countries by showing in an unprecedented way that without addressing the unequal work division between genders, women will continue to have difficulty catching up with men's earnings and financial security.

The OECD has long championed gender equality. Building on this extensive work, the OECD Gender initiative examines existing barriers to gender equality in education, employment and entrepreneurship. The OECD actively promotes policy measures embedded in the 2013 and 2015 OECD Recommendations on Gender Equality in Education, Employment, Entrepreneurship and Public Life. These include measures to ensure access to good quality education for boys and girls, policies to improve the gender balance in leadership in the public sector and providing fathers and mothers equally with financial incentives to use parental leave and flexible work options.

The flagship 2012 publication *Closing the Gender Gap: Act Now!* and the 2017 report *The Pursuit of Gender Equality: An Uphill Battle* assessed policies to promote gender equality in different countries. These country reviews have informed novel policy initiatives like *NiñaSTEM PUEDEN*, which the OECD and the Mexican Ministry of Education jointly launched. The OECD's online Gender Data Portal has become a leading global source for statistical indicators on female education, employment, entrepreneurship, political participation, and social and economic outcomes. The OECD Development Centre's Social Institutions and Gender Index (SIGI) measures discrimination against women in social institutions across 180 countries

The OECD was also instrumental in defining the target adopted by G20 Leaders at their 2014 Brisbane Summit to reduce the gender gap in labour force participation by 25% in 2025. The OECD continues to work closely with G20 and G7 Presidencies on monitoring progress with reducing gender gaps such as these.

Informed by these initiatives, *Gender Equality in Chile* puts forward a comprehensive policy strategy for greater gender equality in the country. The first part of the report reviews the evidence on gender gaps in economic and educational outcomes and on the related possible drivers, including gender attitudes and the distribution of unpaid work. The second part develops a comprehensive framework of policies to allow an equal distribution of paid and unpaid work between men and women and to increase women's labour income. It presents a broad range of viable options to make it easier for couples to equally share unpaid work, to reduce the overall unpaid work burden falling on women and to increase women's labour income.

The final part integrates the effects of the COVID-19 crisis and addresses how the policy priorities of the government have changed to take into account these effects.

The objectives of *Gender Equality in Chile* align to Goal 5 of the UN Sustainable Development Goals for a better and more sustainable future for all, which contemplates achieving gender equality and empowering all women and girls. In particular, Goal 5.4 states the importance to "*Recognize and value unpaid care and domestic work through the provision of public services, infrastructure and social protection policies and the promotion of shared responsibility within the household and the family as nationally appropriate.*"

Acknowledgements

This report is part of a series of country projects within the OECD programme of work on *Gender Equality in Latin America: Towards a better sharing of paid and unpaid work*. The report has been produced with the financial and substantive assistance of the European Union (EU), as part of the Regional Facility for Development in Transition.

The OECD team is grateful to the Ministry of Women and Gender Equity (*Ministerio de la Mujer y la Equidad de Género*) for its invaluable guidance, inputs and comments throughout the project and for its help in convening and organising the OECD mission to Santiago De Chile and subsequent virtual consultations. The team would in particular like to thank Mónica Zalaquett, Minister of Women and Gender Equity, María José Abud, Under Secretary of the Ministry of Women and Gender Equity, María José Díaz, Head of Research Division, Stefania Doebbel, Head of International Affairs Department, Evelyn Larenas and Claudia González, Research Analysts at the Research Division. We would also like to thank Marta Bonet, Deputy Permanent Representative of Chile to the OECD, for her continuous support to facilitate the liaison between the Ministry's team and the OECD team.

The OECD *Gender Equality in Latin America* project is a horizontal effort involving the OECD Global Relations and the OECD Directorate for Employment, Labour and Social Affairs. José Antonio Ardavín, Head of the Latin America and the Caribbean Division, OECD Global Relations Secretariat and Alessandro Goglio, Head of Partner Countries, Directorate for Employment, Labour and Social Affairs, provided co-ordination and support.

The report was prepared by Alessandro Goglio (project leader), Sarah Kups, OECD Directorate for Employment, Labour and Social Affairs and Sofia Blamey Andrusco, OECD Global Relations. Stefano Scarpetta, Director for OECD Employment, Labour and Social Affairs Directorate, Mark Pearson, Deputy Director for OECD Employment, Labour and Social Affairs Directorate, Monika Queisser, Senior Counsellor, Directorate for Employment, Labour and Social Affairs and leader of the OECD Horizontal Project on Gender Equality, Andreas Schaal, Director of OECD Global Relations, all provided strategic oversight for the project, as well as comments. Lorenzo Pavone, Hyeshin Park, Alejandra Maria Meneses and Pierre De Boisséon (OECD Development Centre), Marta Encinas-Martin and Yuri Belfali (OECD Directorate for Education and Skills), Carlos Conde and Gaëlle Ferrant (OECD Global Relations) and the Editorial Board of the OECD Global Relations provided helpful comments to the draft report.

Vanessa Berry Chatelain, Sébastien Mefflet, Julie Whitelock, Yomaira Lopez and Ana Lucía Soto (OECD Global Relations), Brigitte Beyeler and Lucy Hulett (OECD Directorate for Employment, Labour and Social Affairs), provided invaluable support for mission organisation, report layout and design, publication planning, proofreading and editorial support.

The OECD wishes to express sincere gratitude to the EU Facility for Development in Transition in Latin America and the Caribbean, for its support and financial contribution to this project.

Table of contents

FIGURES

TABLES

Follow OECD Publications on:

http://twitter.com/OECD_Pubs

http://www.facebook.com/OECDPublications

http://www.linkedin.com/groups/OECD-Publications-4645871

http://www.youtube.com/oecdilibrary

http://www.oecd.org/oecddirect/

Executive summary

Over the past decades, gender equality in Chile has advanced along several important dimensions. Educational attainments have significantly improved from one age group to the next for both men and women and today, young women out-perform young men in terms of educational outcomes. The share of tertiary graduates is higher among young women than among young men, with slightly higher returns to education for women.

Notwithstanding these achievements, fundamental social and economic gender gaps persist. The traditional male breadwinner *vis-a-vis* female homeworker divide is still common in Chile, meaning that women typically spend more hours looking after children and doing housework. As a result, the combined paid and unpaid working hours of employed women exceeds that of employed men by 12 additional hours of weekly work. Even if women expanded their work outside of the home, they would likely continue doing many tasks commonly perceived as 'women's work', given existing attitudes and stereotypes.

The unequal partition of working hours and tasks affects women and men's economic success. The female employment rate in Chile is almost 20 percentage points lower than the male rate, a gap much wider than the average of the OECD countries. Motherhood has a strong impact and, although mothers of young children generally only withdraw temporarily from the labour market, they will more likely work part-time or informally when they return.

When women do work in Chile, they earn significantly less than men do. The proportion of women who earn a low-income is about 1.6 times as high as that of men in Chile and women are less likely to advance to management. While many young women now obtain more years of schooling than young men do, girls are much less likely to study in the lucrative science, technology, engineering and mathematics (STEM) fields.

The COVID-19 pandemic has brought to light pre-existing challenges in an unprecedented way. Four-fifths of all Chilean women who stopped working during the pandemic did not search for re-employment. Eventually, this massive fallout on labour market inactivity reflects the fact that many women took on even more caring work. It has sparked stress and mental health problems and an upsurge of episodes of violence against women.

The OECD review of *Gender Equality in Chile* puts forward a comprehensive policy strategy for tackling gender inequalities. First, it calls for the provision of sound policies that aim at reducing the barriers that stand in the way of a more equal allocation of time and responsibilities between men and women. Second, it argues that there is room for increasing the participation of women in the labour market by ensuring that women's paid work pays more. Finally, it looks at how the COVID-19 pandemic has uncovered the extent of pre-existing challenges.

Main recommendations for reducing barriers to sharing paid and unpaid work more equitably:

- Create a more comprehensive care system by expanding formal early childhood education and after-school care and by investing in long-term care.

- Expand parental leave by establishing reserved paternity leave weeks as part of parental leave. At the same time, increasing the coverage of maternity and paternity benefits requires the back-up of broader policies to foster formalisation.

- Strengthen flexible work options by allowing for more adaptable starting times and teleworking to reduce the time crunch experienced by parents due to long working hours, commutes and family obligations.

- Continue the efforts to reduce the transmission of gender stereotypes in education both through training to help teachers become more mindful about gender attitudes and stereotypes, and engage the families in the process of creating gender-sensitive education.

Main recommendations for making women's paid work pay more:

- Ensure access to quality education for all by providing additional support to vulnerable girls and teenage mothers and by rewarding and communicating the benefits of completing studies.

- Keep on with the effort to promote women in leadership positions by strengthening women's representation at the executive level, particularly in private sector companies. This should be enhanced by stepping up monitoring and evaluation mechanisms of equal opportunities and equal pay for equivalent work.

- Step up efforts to encourage girls' interest in non-traditional careers such as science, technology and mathematics (STEM), including with the support of mentorship programmes and more efforts to disseminate positive role models.

- Support female entrepreneurship by revamping the reform of the marital law. This requires the abolition of the default rule, which, by foreseeing that the husband administers the marital property, reduces the wife's capacity to raise collateral.

- Fight violence against women by lowering the barriers that prevent the victims of violence and harassment to access the justice system, while at the same time encouraging and guaranteeing safe complaint processes for victims.

Responding to the COVID-19 pandemic:

- Facilitate access of low-income households – in particular single parents, who are predominantly female – to benefits, as well as to social security programmes, which support families as a whole and allow women return to formal employment.

- Prevent women's activity and exclusion from the formal workforce from increasing further by actively informing firms about how to reduce working hours and allow flexible work options, provide relief for working parents, and manage redundancy payments related to temporary lay-offs and sick leave.

- Step up access to emergency measures to self-employed women, especially those who do not qualify for employment insurance.

- Continue the efforts to push back on social acceptance of domestic violence by drawing attention to how the issue affects women and children in confinement. The actions to foster the introduction of electronically-based modes of communication to seek help and report abuse should be complemented by measures to ensure that service delivery for victims is accessible and integrated across the country and relevant spheres.

The above economic and social policy measures must be embedded in a broader effort to mainstream gender in governments' responses to the COVID-19 crisis. In the short run, this means, wherever possible, applying a gender lens to emergency policy measures. In the longer run, it means government having in place a well-functioning system of gender mainstreaming, relying on ready access to gender-disaggregated evidence in all sectors so that differential effects on women and men can be readily assessed.

1 Gender gaps in Chile: An international and sub-national comparison

This chapter reviews the evidence on gender gaps in economic and educational outcomes in Chile and discusses the drivers of these gaps. It starts with an overview of gender gaps in educational and labour market outcomes across different dimensions (enrolment and out-of-school rates, skills outcomes, along with labour market participation, gender pay gaps and the interactions between motherhood and access to job quality). It then discusses the factors contributing to these gaps (unpaid work, attitudes, legal barriers, the role played by violence and access to care facilities). In addition to comparing Chile with other Latin American countries and the OECD, the chapter addresses the articulation of gender differences across socio-economic groups. This includes paying attention to the analysis of urban *vis-à-vis* rural differences, along with differences across levels of education, age and levels of incomes.

Over the past few decades, Chile has made impressive strides in boosting the educational achievements of children and of girls, in particular. Today, the number of young adults of either sex who do not progress to at least an upper secondary degree is as small in Chile as the average across the OECD. Moreover, a slightly higher share of young women than men are university graduates. Women increasingly participate in the labour market and, although the difference between male and female employment rates remains more pronounced than across the OECD, it is not necessarily larger than in other Latin American countries.

In Chile, however, just as in other Latin American countries and all around the world, much remains to be done to narrow gender gaps and ensure the benefits of a more equitable division of paid and unpaid work for family well-being and human capital development (see Box 1.1). Chilean women are less likely to work for pay, especially full-time. Instead, they typically spend more hours looking after children and the elderly, doing housework, shopping for food, cooking, and so on.

This unequal partition of paid and unpaid labour is not merely an equal trade by which women exchange one "unit" of unpaid work for one "unit" of paid work by their partners. In fact, across the OECD, but even more drastically in Chile and Latin America at large, women's total work burden – that is the overall number of paid and unpaid working hours combined – exceeds that of men by a large margin. Moreover, gender inequalities vary widely across socio economic groups – between younger and older generations, between urban and rural areas, between indigenous and non-indigenous populations and between parents and single parents.

This chapter reviews the background in which gender gaps unfold in Chile and their effects on the sharing of paid and unpaid work responsibilities. It describes gender gaps in educational and labour outcomes, along with time-sharing and earning trends, seeking to identify areas in Chile where there has and has not been progress. The chapter also looks at international indicators of well-being and gender gaps that relate to the influence of stereotypes and discrimination and includes a discussion of violence against women.

Gender gaps in education and labour market outcomes

Education

There is an extensive body of research and literature focussing on the importance of education for individuals and society. This shows that individuals with higher levels of education typically have a higher probability of being employed, earning a higher income (OECD, 2019[1]) and being healthier (Conti, Heckman and Urzua, 2010[2]; Dávila-Cervantes and Agudelo-Botero, 2019[3]). At the societal level, the return on the investment in education reflects mainly the enhanced contribution to productivity growth generated by a more educated labour force (Mincer, 1984[4]).

In the case of women, these benefits are even greater. They materialise in terms of decreased child mortality and unwanted pregnancy, along with increased productive capabilities and income opportunities for a group whose ties with the labour market becomes stronger (Woodhall, 1973[5]; Montenegro and Patrinos, 2014[6]) and less discriminated due to its sex (Dougherty, 2005[7]). In addition, and importantly, inter-generational redistribution will improve, since the increased education of mothers typically leads to improved health and education outcomes of their children, even when taking into account the father's education and household income (Schultz, 1993[8]). Furthermore, by making women feel more empowered to speak out to affirm their needs and aspirations, higher levels of education for girls represent a cornerstone of stronger political voice and representation (Marcus and Page, 2016[9]).

There is evidence suggesting that the benefits of increased levels of male and, especially, female education have been widespread in Chile. For example in 2011, the private economic returns to female education were slightly higher than observed for Chilean men. This marked a reversal compared to prior decades: indeed, in the late 1980s, the income boost for men who earned a primary or a tertiary degree, compared to those who did not graduate, was significantly larger than for women (Montenegro and Patrinos, 2014[6]).

Box 1.1. The benefits of a more equitable division of paid and unpaid labour between men and women

Individuals working outside the home generally have a higher degree of economic independence from their partners and other family members than those who do not. Unpaid care and domestic work is also valuable, but in general does not garner the same societal recognition as other activities do. In countries where they carry out a disproportionally large share of the unpaid work burden, women are more frequently in part-time or vulnerable, often poorly paid, jobs (Ferrant, Pesando and Nowacka, 2014[10]). This is because high unpaid care and domestic work burdens often imply that women cannot find an occupation corresponding to their qualification level on a part-time basis, which decreases job quality and earnings (Connolly and Gregory, 2008[11]).

By contrast, an equal division of unpaid labour can benefit the entire family. High work hours can lead to stress, and to the extent that a more equal sharing of unpaid work reduces women's overall work hours – in particular regarding tasks that are considered less desirable, namely housework and care of the elderly – can reduce stress levels (MacDonald, Phipps and Lethbridge, 2005[12]). A study of British families suggests that couples in which men do more unpaid care and other housework are less likely to divorce (Sigle-Rushton, 2010[13]). The negative effects of an unequal division of unpaid work on marital quality are particularly strong when couples disagree about how egalitarian a marriage should be (Ogolsky, Dennison and Monk, 2014[14]). Men who spend more time with their children may have higher life satisfaction and their children may have better mental and physical health and cognitive development. However, it is unclear whether these results are driven by confounding factors not accounted for in these studies. (WHO, 2007[15]).

Individuals' well-being may be boosted even further if overall unpaid care and domestic work hours can be reduced. When an increasing share of the population is able to access stable utilities (such as running water and electricity) and labour-saving appliances (such as washing machines) and thus need fewer hours for housework, this reduces time-poverty and increases choices. As a result, in countries with higher GDP levels, the number of hours that need to be devoted to unpaid work decrease, benefitting women in particular (Ferrant and Thim, 2019[16]).

An increased participation of women in paid compared to unpaid work likely increases economic growth. The impact would go far beyond an accounting 'trick' of simply substituting unpaid by paid work: an estimation based on the 2015 time-use survey suggests that in Chile, unpaid domestic work contributes 22% of a modified GDP measure (INEI, 2016[17]); (Comunidad Mujer, 2020[17]). Women's increased participation in the labour market would substitute lower- for higher-added value activities and increase the stock of human capital employed. Since young female university graduates now outnumber their male counterparts, using their human capital fully has become more urgent. Moreover, firm-level research suggests that teams that are more diverse may be more cohesive and innovative. This suggests that bringing more women into the labour market, including into management positions, could increase productivity and economic growth.

Moreover, educational levels of men and women in Chile have increased consistently over time and in tandem from one cohort to the next. Although less than half of men and women aged 55-64 had achieved at least an upper secondary degree in 2017, the same share among young adults three decades younger had risen to 83.5% and 86.8% for men and women, respectively (Figure 1.1).

Furthermore and importantly, the recent figures point to young women having started to out-perform young men in terms of educational attainments: Among 25-34 year-olds, the share of tertiary graduates is higher among women than men (36.9% compared to 30.3%). In contrast, in the middle age categories (35-54), the educational attainments of men and women are very similar.

Figure 1.1. More young women than men in Chile attain tertiary degrees

Highest educational attainment by sex and age (% of population in age group), 2018

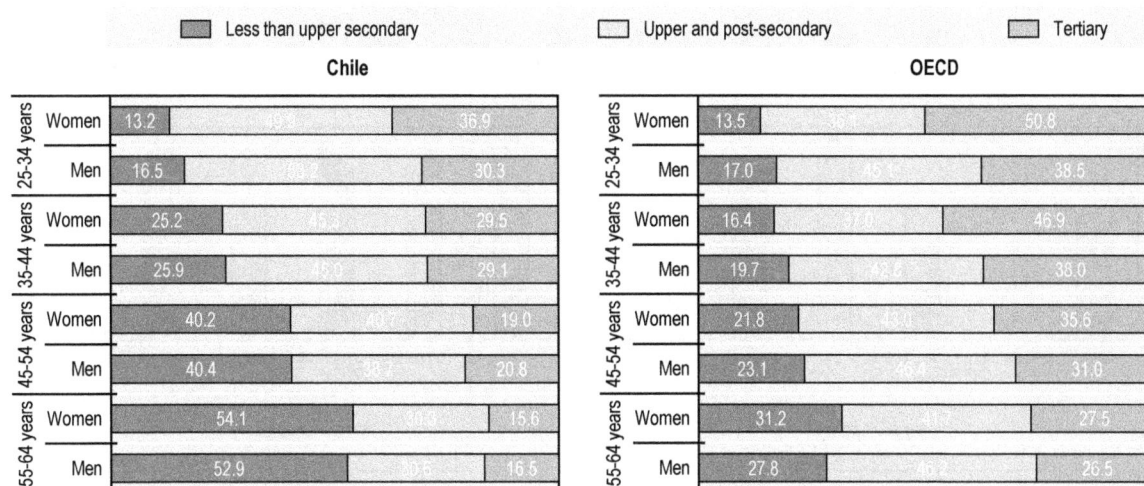

Source: OECD (2019[1]), *Education at a Glance* and UNESCO Institute for Statistics Database (n.d.[18]), http://data.uis.unesco.org/.

Enrolment rates and early drop-outs

Access to schooling within a population can vary across age groups and between genders. In Chile, the enrolment rates of boys and girls in pre-primary and primary education are virtually identical (Figure 1.2). Later on, however, the share of teenage girls who enrol is higher than the share of boys, which mirrors a pattern across many other Latin American and OECD countries. Since not all officially enrolled children regularly attend school, educational experts and observers are generally wary of establishing a direct relationship between the increase in the number of enrolments and the progress in education achievements. Nevertheless, parallel to the rise of school enrolments, Chile has experienced a decline of inadequate reading and writing skills across the population, implying, as a result, that today's illiteracy rates are also very similar: in 2017, the Chilean share of illiterate individuals was 3.5% among men and 3.7% among women (Observatorio Social, 2018[19]). However, results from the Survey of Adult Skills (PIAAC) show that more than one in two Chilean adults (53.4%) in 2015 had only a low literacy proficiency level. This result was similar to Mexico, although better than in other countries in the region, such as Ecuador and Peru, for example (OECD, 2019[20]).

It is worth emphasising, however, that the average figures mask important differences across socio-economic groups. For example, the illiteracy rate is significantly lower than the national average among Chilean youth (15-29 year-old, 1.1%). At the same time, it is much higher in rural areas (8.3%) and among individuals who are in the two lowest quintiles of the income distribution (7.1 and 4.5%, respectively). In addition, the average years of schooling are substantially lower in rural areas: among the population aged 15 and above in 2017, the urban population on average had 11.5 years of schooling and the rural population 8.9 years. The gap between indigenous and non-indigenous populations was slightly less than one year (Observatorio Social, 2018[19]). PIAAC results show that among younger adults aged 16 to 24, women outperform men in terms of average literacy scores; while the opposite is true in the 25-44 and in particular 45-65 year-old age categories (OECD, 2019[20]).

Figure 1.2. Chilean teenage girls are more frequently enrolled in school than Chilean boys are

Net enrolment rates, 2018 or latest

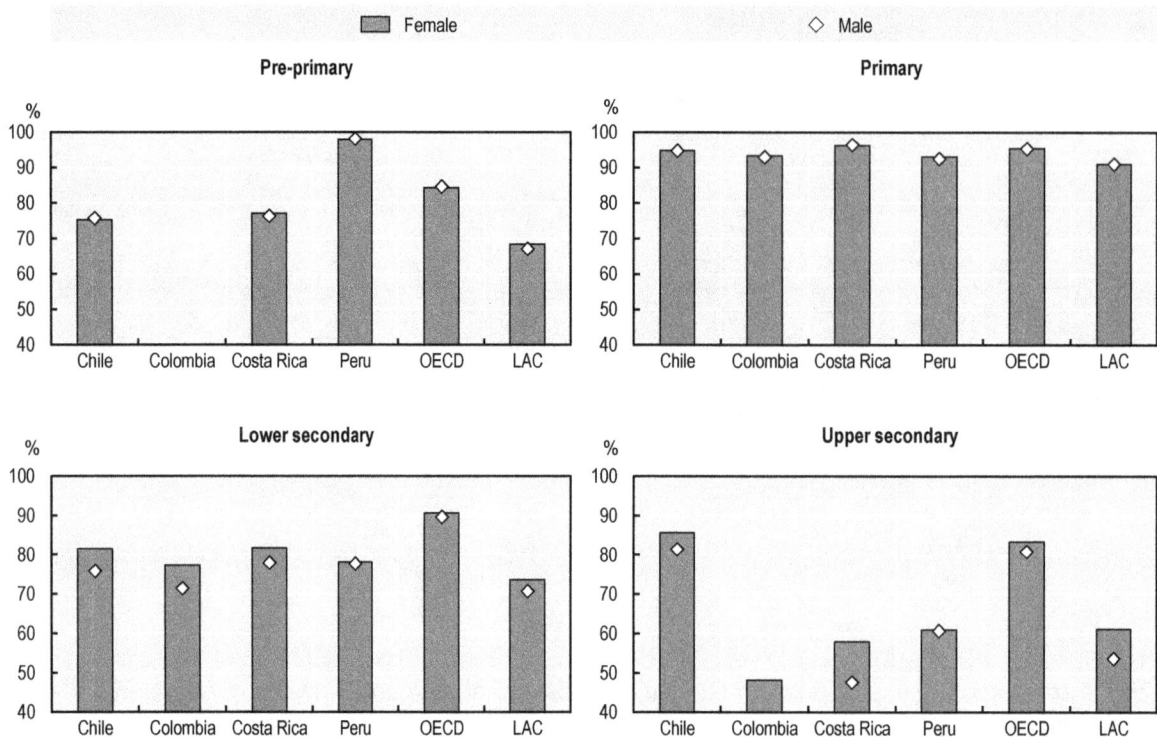

Source: UNESCO Institute for Statistics Database (n.d.[18]), "Net enrolment rate", http://data.uis.unesco.org/.

Evidence indicates that in Chile school dropouts relate closely to the socio-economic background of the students (MINEDUC, 2020[21]; Observatorio Social, 2018[19]). Students from disadvantaged households tend to change schools more frequently, which threatens their curriculum progression. Early school leavers are over-represented among the groups of youth who combine several disadvantages, typically economic difficulties with pre-existing family difficulties. Furthermore, one key reason typically advanced by individuals from remote areas, whether rural or decentralised urban neighborhoods, is the lack of proximity to the education institutions. Students at higher risks of drop put are also typically more exposed to contiguity stressors, such as the fact of living in a high crime area (MINEDUC, 2020[21]).

Figure 1.3 looks at the decomposition of children not enrolled in school by sex. In Chile, the share of out-of-school children is higher among girls than among boys at the primary and lower secondary level and virtually identical among upper secondary school age teenagers (Observatorio Social, 2018[19]). This sets Chile somewhat apart in the international comparison, given that in the average of the Latin American countries out-of-school rates tend to be higher among boys, particularly at the pre-primary and upper secondary school age.

Figure 1.3. The rate of out-of-school teenagers in Chile is comparatively low

Rate of out-of-school children by age group (% of children in age group), 2018 or latest available

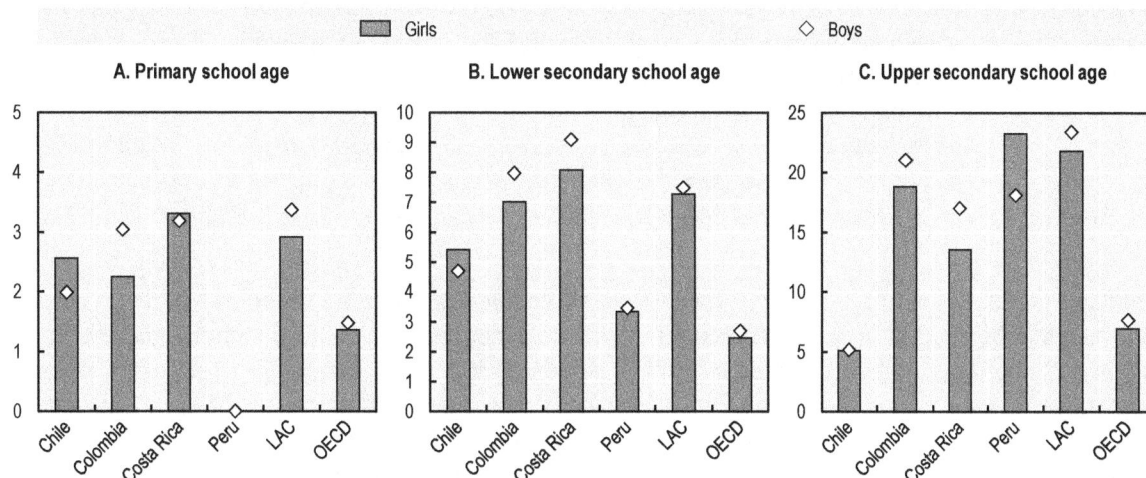

Note: Based on administrative enrolment data at a given point in time.
Source: UNESCO Institute for Statistics Database (n.d.[18]), "Out of School Children", http://data.uis.unesco.org/.

Additional insights into the factors that influence access to education are attainable by looking at the work obligations of teenagers outside school. In Chile in 2012, 3.8% of 5-14 year-olds and 16.5% of 15-17 year-olds were working, with the number of boys being more than twice than among girls (ILO, MINTRAB and MINDESARROLLO, 2013[22]). That said, the evidence available also shows that girls aged 12 to 17 work more hours in unpaid care and domestic activities than boys of the same age do.

Working outside school does not necessarily lead to worse educational outcomes, but working many hours does, unless a strict and effective regulation preventing the excess work of teenagers applies. The results of a standardised test, shows that students in Chile who work tend to perform worse than their peers who do not. (Post, 2011[23]). Interestingly, the negative effects held for the reading test score and increased between the first and third hour of work per day, after which the negative effect flattened. The author of the study speculates that this apparently odd result could reflect the enforcement of the law against the work of teenagers (Post, 2011[23]). In a study based on 20 countries, both paid and unpaid work outside of school are seen to negatively affect maths scores of girls and boys, even when family resources and school effects are taken into account (Post and Pong, 2009[24]).

Teenage pregnancy

In many countries, teenage pregnancy and the child caregiving responsibilities that result from it imply that it is very difficult for teenage mothers to finish school. Importantly, teenage mothers often have to leave school under pressure from the family or even the school's management, because of shame and stigma. Women who have become mothers before the age of 20 usually report significantly less years of schooling and less work hours than women with delayed childbearing (Arceo-Gomez and Campos-Vazquez, 2014[25]) (Publimetro, 2018[26]).

Adults who had children during their teenage years usually belong to those groups with the lowest levels of reading and writing proficiency (OECD, 2018[27]). Across the countries covered by the PIAAC survey, about 16% of women aged 20 to 65 years old who are in the lowest quintile of literacy scores became mothers in their teens, compared to 4% in the highest quintile. Among female teenagers, a low literacy level associates to a higher probability of motherhood: 6% of women aged 16-19 in the lowest quintile of the national literacy score distribution are mothers, compared to almost none for the most proficient women at the same age (Jonas and Thorn, 2018[28]).

Chile has registered improvements in this area of prominent importance for the fight against poverty and raising equality of opportunities (UNESCO, 2014[29]). The share of teenage mothers has dropped by half since the turn of the millennium, from 16.2% of all births to 7.9% in 2017 (Sepúlveda, 2019[30]). Estimates for 2012 indicate that the fertility rate – the number of births per 1 000 girls in the age group – was 1.4 for girls aged between 10 and 14 years and 48.6 for 15-19 year-olds, respectively (MINSAL, 2013[31]). Although, the rate was the lowest in Latin America and the situation may have improved further in the past years, it was four times higher than the OECD average. In addition, it is worth noting that the rate in the Latin American region is second only to the Sub-Saharan African region (PAHO, UNFPA and UNICEF, 2017[32]).

In addition, teenage mothers are typically over-represented among adolescents of disadvantaged backgrounds (ECLAC, 2017[33]). This represents a source of concern in Chile, given that in the country the proportion of teenage mothers is three times higher among the most vulnerable households than it is among the least vulnerable (31.4% and 10.6% respectively) (Observatorio Social, 2017[34]). In addition to dramatically hampering mothers' economic prospects, the poverty and inequality consequences of teenage motherhood are intergenerational. Babies born to women under 20 years of age are more likely to be preterm or to have a low birth weight, and the rate of neonatal mortality is comparatively high for these babies (NEAL, 2018[35]).

Skills outcomes

The results of the OECD Survey of Adult Skills – the Programme for the International Assessment of Adult Competencies, PIAAC – provide key information on the skills of the adult population (16-65) in participating countries. Men in Chile have higher average numeracy and literacy skills than women do, with the extent of the (unadjusted) gender gaps being second only to Turkey among OECD countries. The fact that men have higher average literacy scores than women is surprising on account of the fact that gender differences in literacy scores are typically not statistically significant in most countries (OECD, 2016[36]). One possible explanation of this puzzle is that, reflecting family domestic and care obligations, many women spend long periods without working in paid employment. These career interruptions lead them, in turn, to lose part of their skills. Some evidence in support of this stems from the fact that among 16-24 year-olds – an age interval during which many young women graduates are employed in a paid job, thanks to less compelling family obligations – the literacy skills of women exceed those of men.

The OECD's Programme for International Student Assessment (PISA) provides complementary "food for thought", by allowing inspecting the education achievements of teenagers who are still in school. Importantly, the results of the PISA survey show a lower presence of low performers in reading among girls than boys, with the gap being comparable to that across the OECD and larger than in other Latin American countries (Figure 1.4). Nevertheless, in Chile the share of low achievers in maths among girls is higher than observed among boys, though less so than in other Latin American countries.

Figure 1.4. There are gender differences in the share of low but not of top performers in the PISA study in Chile

Difference in the share of low achievers and top performers by subject (girls – boys), 2018

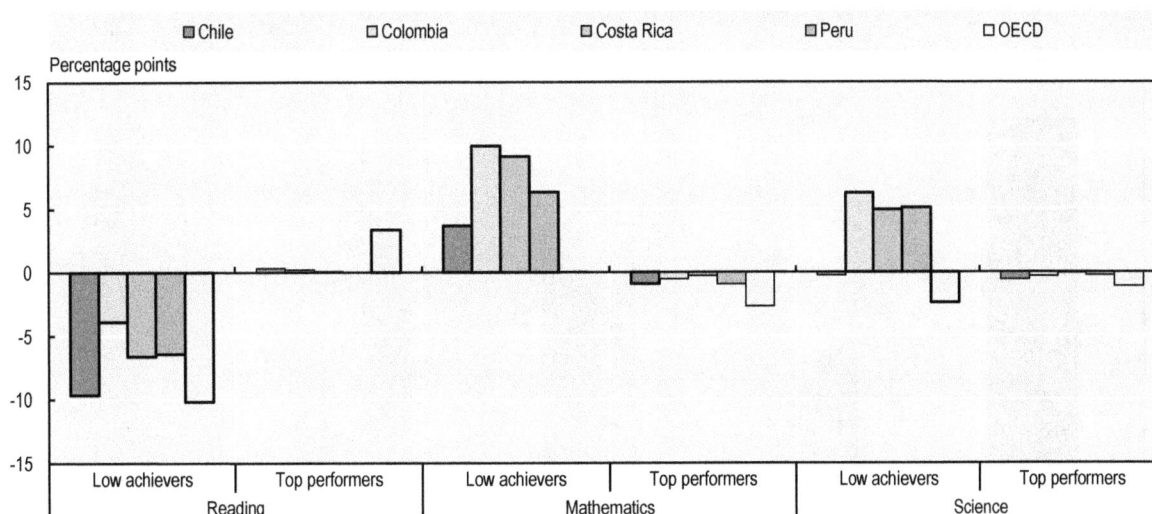

Note: Bars with bold outlines indicate that the gender difference is statistically significant.
Source: OECD (2019[37]), *PISA 2018 Results (Volume II)*, Annex B1, Tables II.B1.7.12, 17 and 22.

Taken together, the above results signal that, during their teenage years, Chilean girls may have already developed a disposition towards academic disciplines in the sphere of humanities, rather than the scientific spheres, which instead tend to be seen as a prerogative of teenage boys. This divergence has a counterpart in the choices that girls and boys will make later on, first as students, later on as workers. The analysis of the decomposition by sex of the graduates in science, technology, engineering, and mathematics – the so-called STEM subjects – allows shedding some light into this issue. In particular, the analysis of the shares of men and women graduates in STEM subjects reveals that in 2017, the gender gap in Chile was larger than the OECD average and much larger than the comparator Latin American countries (Figure 1.5).

Several factors explain the performance differences in quantitative subjects between girls and boys. Some refer to aptitudes, although score differences in math tests are negligible among small children, and others to preferences (Kahn and Ginther, 2018[38]). Yet, it is clear that gender stereotypes contribute to these differences (Nollenberger, Rodríguez-Planas and Sevilla, 2016[39]). As discussed in the second part of this report, the latter is an important aspect that gender-sensitive education aims to address (see the section on "Reducing gender stereotypes").

Figure 1.5. The gender gap in STEM graduates is particularly stark in Chile

Share of graduates in STEM subjects (% graduates of same gender), 2017

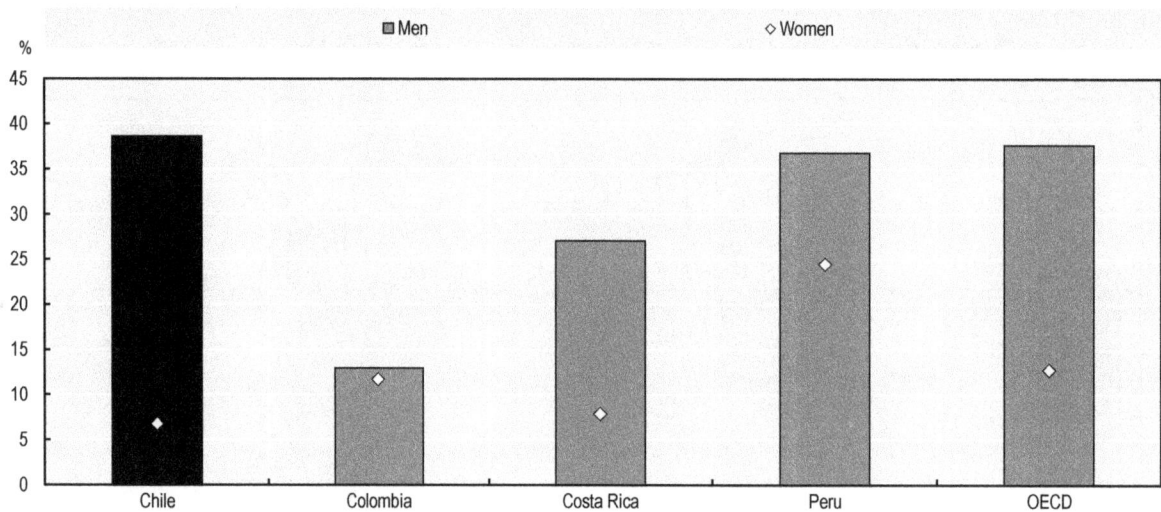

Note: All tertiary levels combined. STEM subjects include natural sciences, mathematics, statistics, information and communication technologies, engineering, manufacturing and construction.
Source: OECD (2019[1]), *Education at a Glance* and UNESCO Institute for Statistics Database (UNESCO Institute for Statistics, n.d.[18]).

Employment

Educational choices and the qualifications attained are key factors in helping workers find their way into more stable and better quality employment opportunities. In all countries, this way is more difficult to find for women than it is for men, although there are variations from country to country. The evidence available suggests that in Chile the difficulties that women face are greater than in many other OECD countries. At 53.2%, the female rate of employment in Chile is almost 20 percentage points lower than the corresponding male level (Figure 1.6). In addition, this size of the gender gap is wider than the average of the OECD countries, whereas in the comparison with the Latin America countries selected for this analysis, it is wider than in Peru, although less sizeable than observed in Colombia and Costa Rica.

As discussed above, Chile is characterised by the presence of marked differences in educational outcomes between age and socio-economic groups. Against this background, a pertinent question to ask is whether similar variations are detectable in the performance of the labour market. The available evidence confirms that in Chile there are significant gender gaps in employment across age groups. Specifically, the extent of the gender gap appears to be more significant among the older cohorts, which are also characterised by wider gender gaps in education and skills levels. It ranges between 4.0% among 15-24 year-olds to 33.5% among 55-64 year-olds, with continuous increases for each age group in between (OECD, 2018[40]).

A rising gap in the employment rate with age reflects mechanically the fact that fewer women in older generations ever participated in the labour force. In addition to this "cohort effect", there is a "composition effect", because as educational attainments improve more young women with higher degrees of education will find a job. In Chile, fewer than four in ten women who did not complete secondary education participate in the labour market, which compares with more than seven in ten among women with an upper secondary education degree and nearly nine in ten among university graduates.

Figure 1.6. The employment rates of Chilean men and women are comparatively low

Employment-to-population ratio (% 15-64 year-olds), 2018 or latest available

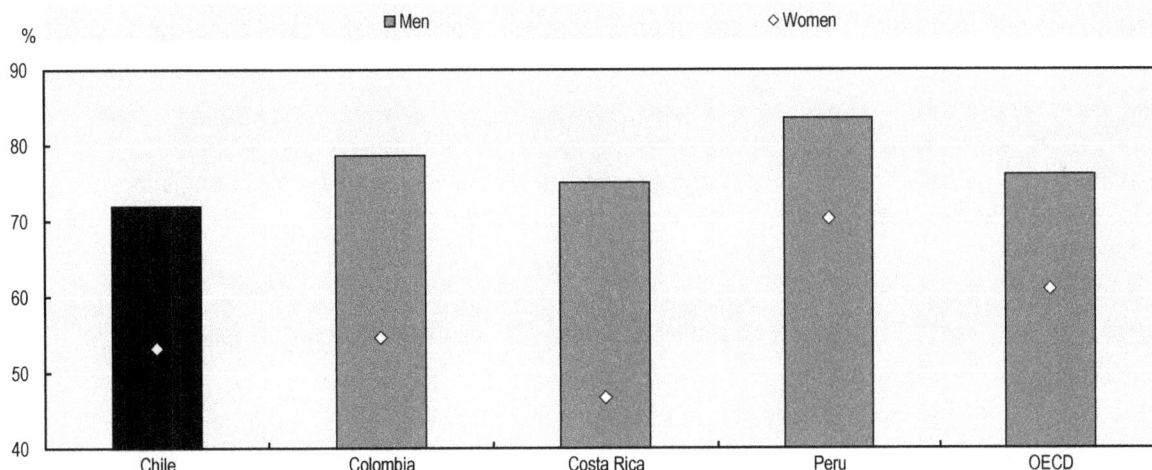

Note: For Peru, the latest available data is from 2017.
Source: OECD Employment Database (OECD, n.d.[41]) and ILOSTAT (ILO, n.d.[42]).

Motherhood and access to job quality

However, in Chile as elsewhere motherhood has a strong impact on the workforce of the younger generations, which is visible in many mothers of young children withdrawing (temporarily) from the labour force (Figure 1.7). In Chile the employment rate of mothers with children below three years old is 10 percentage points lower than the rate of mothers with children aged three to five years and 15 points lower than the rate of mothers whose youngest child is aged between six and 14 years.

Figure 1.7. Mothers have low employment rates in Chile

Maternal employment rates by age of youngest child, 2014 or latest available year

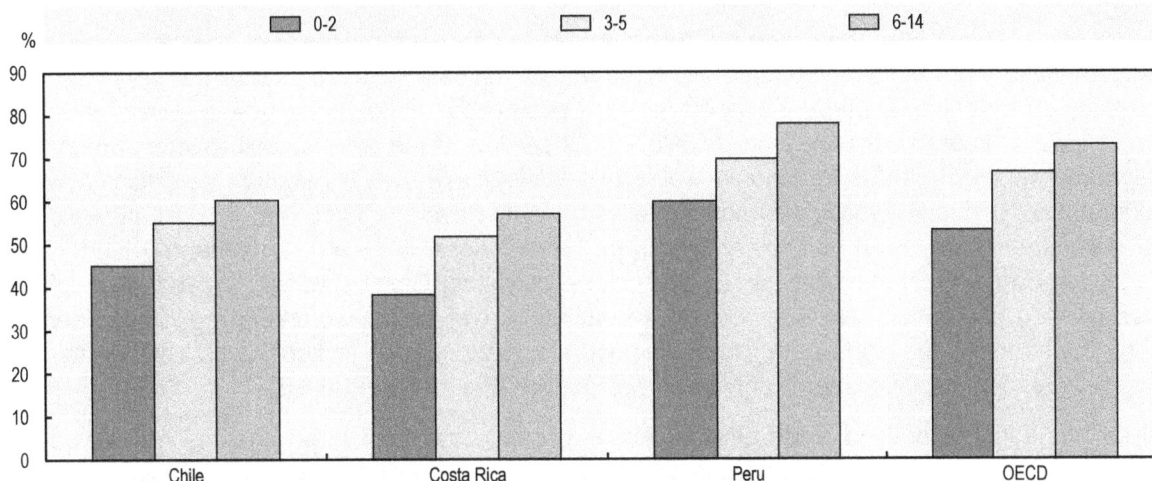

Note: Data for Peru is for 2018, for Costa Rica to 2014, for Chile 2013 and the OECD for the latest available year in 2012-13.
Source: OECD (n.d.[43]), "LMF1.2.C Maternal employment rates by age of youngest child", *OECD Family Database*, http://www.oecd.org/social/family/database.htm; and own estimations based on the INE (2019[44]), *Encuesta Nacional de Hogares*.

Much like in other regional economies, the main challenge faced by women in Chile is not the lack of jobs, since open unemployment is seldom an issue in these countries. Rather, the greatest concerns relate to the lack of quality jobs. Indeed, the evidence available confirms that female workers in Chile are more likely to be in marginal forms of employment than male workers are. For example, the share of part-time workers is around twice as high among women than men (Figure 1.8, Panel A). This level is similar to Colombia and the OECD average, but lower than observed in Costa Rica and Peru.

In addition, the share of informal workers is slightly larger among women than among men in Chile (Figure 1.8, Panel B). Nevertheless, perhaps related to the fact that Chile's per-capita income is higher than in the other comparator countries of Latin America, the female informal employment is lower in Chile than in Costa Rica and significantly lower than in Colombia and Peru. Still it concerns about three in ten employed individuals.

Figure 1.8. A high share of female employees in Chile work part-time and informally

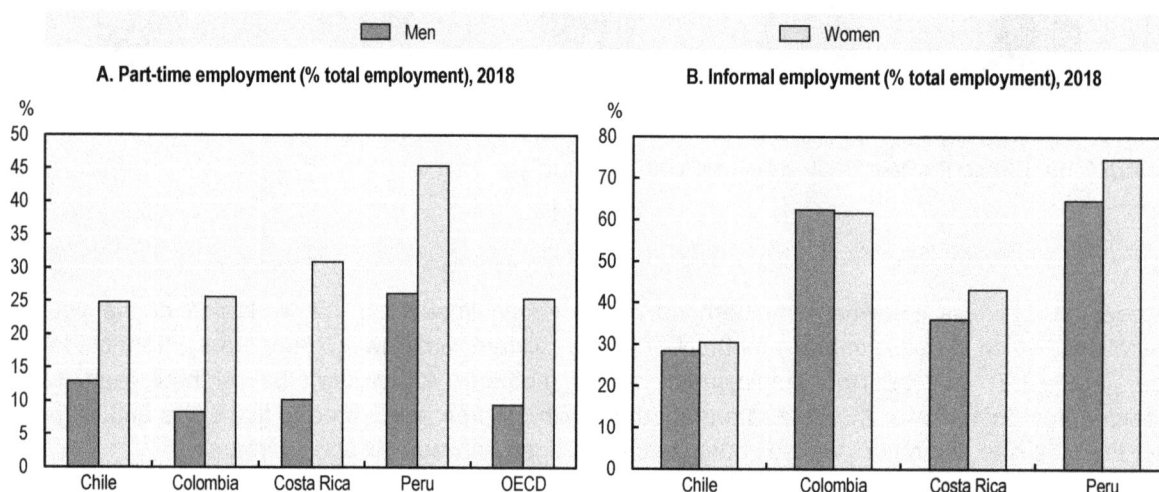

Source: OECD Employment Database (OECD, n.d.[41]) and ILOSTAT (ILO, n.d.[42]).

Entrepreneurship

In all countries, entrepreneurship plays an important role in job creation. However, the demarcation line between necessity-driven entrepreneurs – i.e. those who do not have other employment alternatives –and opportunity-driven entrepreneurs – those moved by a good economic opportunity – is always difficult to draw. As a way of capturing these effects in Chile, Figure 1.9 depicts the comparison between own-account entrepreneurs (Panel A) and entrepreneurs who act as employers (Panel B). Although the indicator of own-account entrepreneurs likely includes representatives of both drivers, a large part of those classified as employer entrepreneurs must be opportunity-driven. Nevertheless, there are signs that moving towards opportunity-driven entrepreneurship can be particularly difficult for Chilean women. Indeed, although the shares of male and female workers who are accounted as own-account workers are almost identical (Figure 1.9, Panel A), the share of employers among employed women is significantly smaller than the same share among employed men – only about half as high (Figure 1.9, Panel B).

Analysis of the individual traits of self-employment and entrepreneurship shows that in Chile the gender gap among entrepreneurs who started a business because they identified a good opportunity, rather than out of necessity, is bigger than on average in Latin America and the Caribbean and in the OECD (Mandakovic et al., 2017[45]). Another recent study finds that the propensity of being in self-employment reflects the expectation of relatively large earnings – compared with being hired as an employee – but this holds true only in the case of entrepreneurs who also act as employers (Modrego, Paredes and Romaní, 2017[46]). The authors conclude that this evidence corroborates the view that in Chile entrepreneurs who are also employers are more likely to choose their occupational status, unlike own account workers who are pushed to into self-employment out of necessity. However, Chilean women entrepreneurs are far more likely to fall into this second category, as suggested by the fact that in Chile in 2020, about 40% of owners of micro-enterprises registered as natural persons companies were women. In contrast, only 25% of medium and 18% of large companies with the same registration form were owned by women (Ministerio de Economia Fomento y Turismo, 2020[47]; Ministerio de Economía Fomento y Turismo, 2017[48]). Women are also under-represented in the general management of large firms (12.8% of posts in 2016), compared to the SMEs (28.9%). Female micro entrepreneurs are more represented in the informal sector than men are (57.3%; as compared to 42.8%) and their companies are significantly less profitable. About 70% of these women earn less than the Chilean minimum wage (CLP 337 000, which is equal to around USD 457) (Ministerio de Economia Fomento y Turismo, 2020[47]).

Figure 1.9. A low share of female entrepreneurs are employers

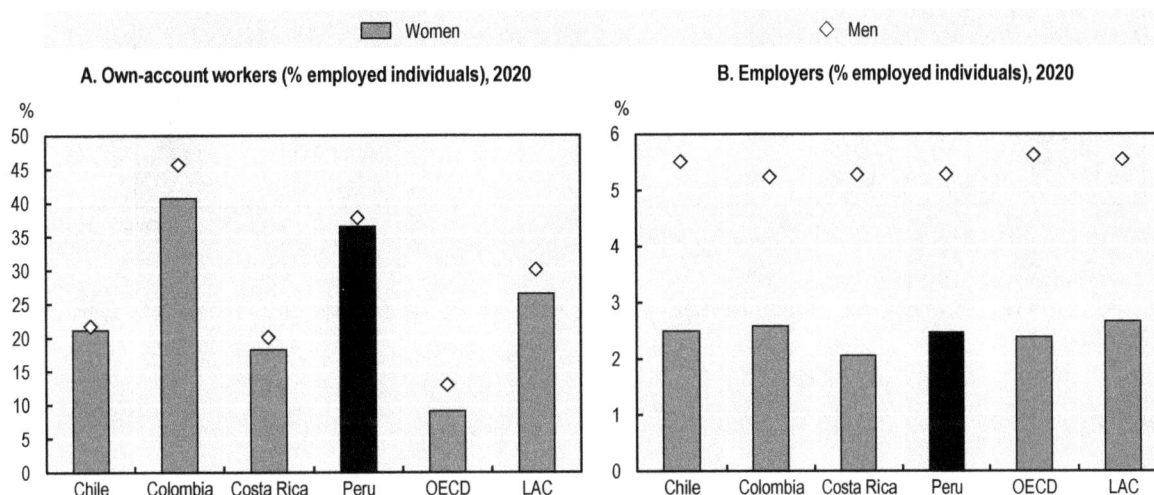

Source: ILO (n.d.[42]), "Employment by sex, rural / urban areas and status in employment – ILO modelled estimates, Nov. 2019 (thousands)", *ILOSTAT*.

Gender pay gaps

One key indicator of inequality between men and women is the gender pay gap. By detecting how much less money the average female worker earns, it allows the drawing of relevant information on the structure of work incentives that women face and their distribution between women and men. As a result, it can affect the choice within the couple as to whether both wife and husband will work full-time, for example.

One simple indicator of the gender pay differences is the prevalence of low-income workers among women and men. In Chile, more than one in seven (13.6%) full-time female workers earn less than two-thirds of the median wage (Figure 1.10). This means that the low-income worker share for women is about 1.6 times as high as the share for men. The relative prevalence of low pay between women and men rate in Chile is comparable to Colombia, Peru and the OECD.

The gap in earnings between male and female employees is higher in Chile than elsewhere. The median wage of male full-time employees is 12% higher than of their female counterparts, similar to the OECD average but a larger gap than in Colombia and Costa Rica (Figure 1.11, OECD estimate).[1] The difference is even larger in an ILO measure of the pay gap that includes both part- and full-time workers and that takes into account different educational levels and shares in public versus private sector employment (Figure 1.11, ILO factor-weighted estimate). One likely explanation for the larger gap implied by the ILO approach is that more women than men work in low paid part-time jobs.

Figure 1.10. In Chile as elsewhere, women are more likely to be low-paid

Share of full-time workers earning less than two-thirds of the median wage, 2017 or the most recently available

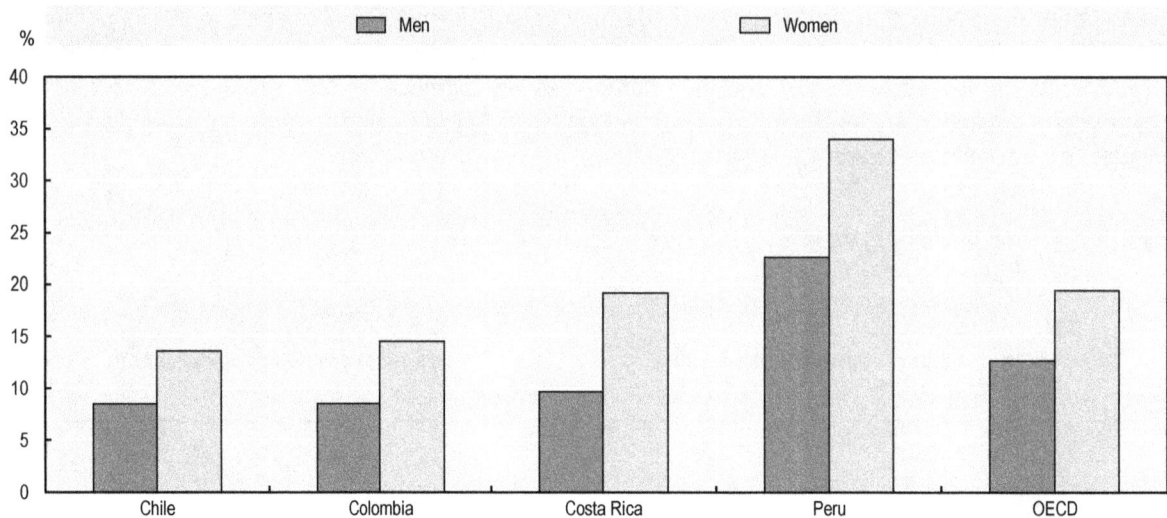

Note: The reference year is 2018 for Colombia and Peru.
Source: OECD (n.d.[49]), *LFS – Decile ratios of gross earnings – Incidence of low pay* and own calculations based on the 2018 annual ENAHO ((INE, 2019[44]).

Figure 1.11. On an hourly basis, the extent of the gender pay gap is particularly high in Chile

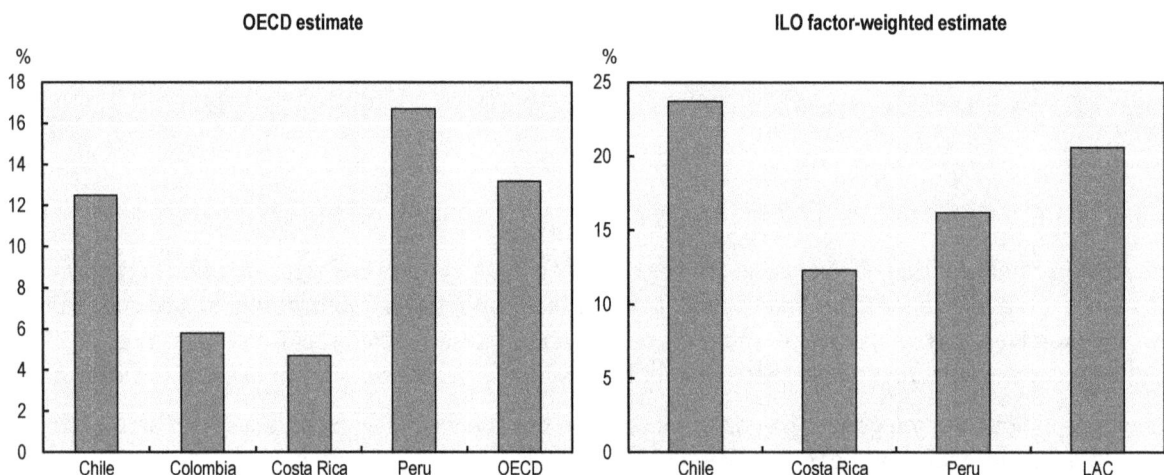

Note: The OECD pay gap is equal to the difference in the median wages of male and female full-time employees. The ILO factor-adjusted pay gap is based on hourly wages and includes both part- and full-time dependent workers. It is equal to a population-size weighted sum of the gender pay gap for different subgroups defined by four education and age groups each, full- and part-time work status and private versus public sector employment.
Source: OECD (n.d.[41]), "Gender wage gap", *Employment Database*, https://stats.oecd.org/index.aspx?queryid=54751; own calculations based on the INE (2019[44]), *Encuesta Nacional de Hogares;* and ILO (2018[50]), *Global Wage Report 2018/19: What lies behind gender pay gaps.*

Leadership positions

The mirror image of the above patterns is the relative under-representation of Chilean women in well-paid occupations positions, including STEM occupations. In part, this reflects the high concentration of female employment in part time jobs in the service sector, rather than full-time jobs in higher added-value activities. In addition, the under-representation of women in well-paid jobs may be a consequence of the above discussed differences in educational background (MINDES, 2018[51]), This includes, for example, the fact that women often shy away from STEM careers, which are more likely to open the way to better paid job opportunities (Figure 1.5). This under-representation of women in STEM education careers implies, in turn, that women are also under-represented in research and academic faculty careers: according to UNESCO, only one in three researchers in Chile are women (UNESCO, 2015[52]). Women make up 41% of doctoral students and receive around 40% of state STEM research scholarships (CONICYT, 2018[53]).

Women in Chile also make little headway in leadership positions in the private sector. Between 1995 and 2018, the share of women who hold high-level leadership positions in six sectors and strategic consulting firms tripled from 3% to 9%. The same is true for board of director posts. As a result, the current share in Chile is still several percentage points below the OECD average (12%) (OECD, 2016[54]), albeit close to the regional average (8.5%) (IDB, 2018[55]). In addition, there appear to be differences in the types of leadership positions held by men and women. Women are under-represented in director, financial and operational roles and over-represented in marketing (33%) and human resources (31%) positions (PNUD, 2020[56]).

Women are better represented in the public sector and politics. In 2020, 48% of public companies' board of directors where women. Information for 2018 show that women held one-quarter political positions in Chile. In the judicial system, public institutions and the executive, their share was even higher, reaching one-third or more of the total (PNUD, 2020[56]). Following the quota law on gender representation at the legislature, in 2018 23% of the members of the Chilean Congress were women, somewhat below the OECD average (23.8%) (OECD, 2017[57]) and well below the regional rate (29.8%) (ECLAC, 2019[58]).

Drivers of gender gaps in outcomes

Various economic theories explain the underlying causes of the above-discussed gender gaps in economic outcomes. The approaches that put the accent on human capital factors emphasise the characteristics of workers and their jobs, particularly the level of education, the work experience and the skills required to fulfil specific tasks and responsibilities. However, human capital characteristics will hardly be enough to capture the wide range of factors explaining gender gaps, if left alone. For example, although education is a leading factor explaining female employment, other factors more intrinsically related to the fact of being a woman are also important to consider. But the roots of the problem go deeper: lacks of qualifications to find a job, the struggle with personal or social problems, for example, are typically intersectional. In other words, they tend to associate with other disadvantages, the fact of being in a young age, of living in a rural area, of coming from a poor household, or of belonging to an indigenous population group.

One synthetic but nevertheless telling manifestation of these complex intersections is provided by Figure 1.12, which depicts the international comparison of the NEET rates for women and men – conventionally defined as the shares of the youth Not in Employment, Education or Training – as a percentage of the youth population. In Chile, young women are 1.6 times more likely to be NEET than young men are. This sizeable gap is slightly larger than the OECD-wide average of 1.5 times, although there are variations from country to country.

The reasons behind this situation are multiple. They may be found in the traditional gender-related assignment of roles, whereby women do most of the unpaid domestic work alongside the caring for children and other family members. Another reason may reflect the influence of inherited cultural factors, gender stereotypes and attitudes and their interplay in influencing the behaviours of men and women. Yet another reason may stem from the role of laws and institutions. Finally, the contribution of infrastructure factors also matters, with the availability of care facilities and of physical infrastructure being one example. The reminder of this section provides a review of these forces, which integrate the role played by human capital factors in shaping gender economic outcomes.

Figure 1.12. Women are more likely to be NEETs than men are

15-29 year-olds not in Employment, Education or Training (% youth population), 2019 or latest available year

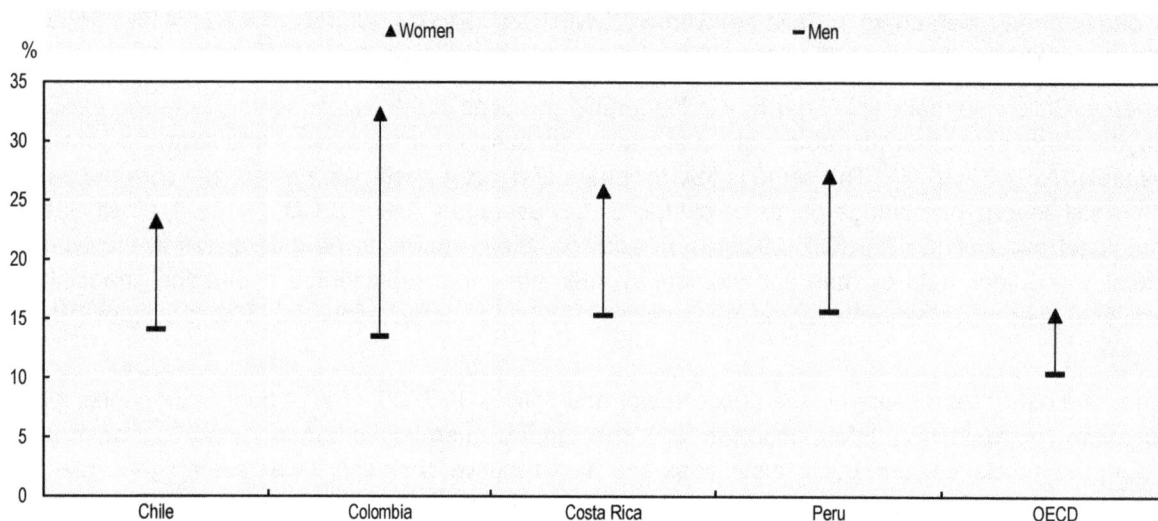

Note: Chile refers to 2017 and Peru to 2016.
Source: Own calculation based on Labour Force Surveys, OECD (2019[59]), *Investing in Youth: Peru* and OECD (2020[60]), *Education at a Glance 2020.*

Unpaid work

The high number of unpaid hours spent on care and housework is one of the main reasons why few women work (full-time) for pay. Recent SIGI data show that on average the time that LAC women spend on unpaid care and domestic work is three times longer than the time spent by men. (OECD, 2020[61]).

In Chile, women on average spend 21 hours more on these tasks than men spend, based on the latest figures available (Figure 1.13, Panel A). The international comparison deserves some caution, since countries may use different approaches to define the population sample. For example, the comparison with the OECD appears limited by the fact that the Chilean indicator focusses on all employed individuals aged 15 years old, or above, whereas the OECD indicator covers the entire population between 15-64 years. This caveat withstanding, the extent of the gap in Chile is wider than the OECD average. By contrast, men work more hours for pay than women do in Chile. At nine hours, the gender gap in paid hours is less than half as large as the gender gap in unpaid hours. In the comparator Latin American countries, as well as the average of the OECD countries, the difference between the two gaps is significantly smaller. Mirroring the image of the adults' representation, teenage girls do more unpaid work and teenage boys more paid work in Chile (Figure 1.13, Panel B).

Figure 1.13. Women and girls in Chile work longer hours than men and boys

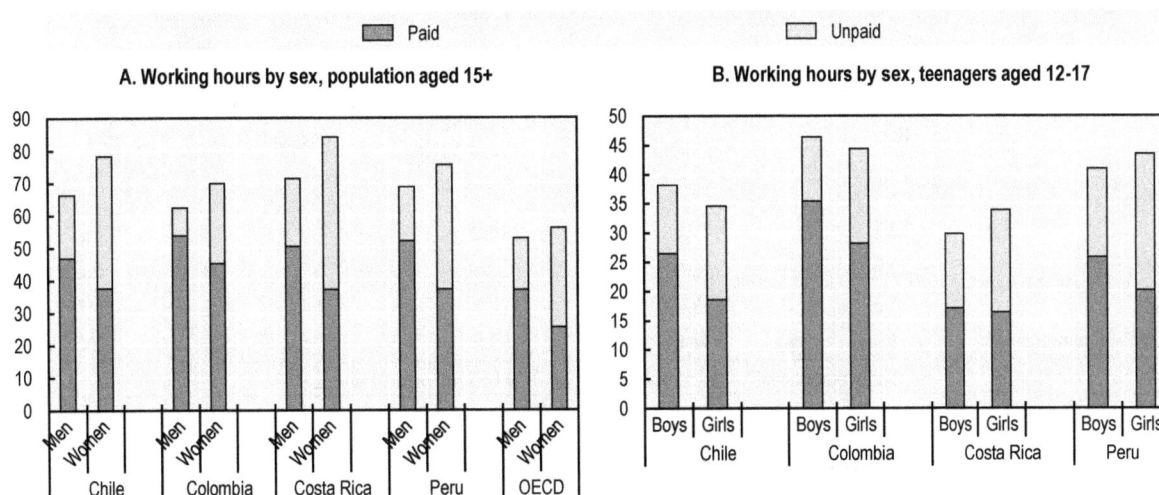

Note: Figure A refers to the population with any paid employment. Given that the survey instruments of the time-use surveys are not identical across countries, more attention should be paid to intra- than to cross-country comparisons. The reference year is 2015 for Chile, 2012 for Colombia, 2011 for Costa Rica, 2010 for Peru and around 2014 for the non-weighted OECD cross-country average. The OECD average refers to the entire population aged 15-64 and is calculated by multiplying daily time use values by seven; and the Colombian average for teenagers refers to 10-17 year-olds.

Source: OECD (2017[62]), *OECD Family Database* and ECLAC (2018[63]), *Los cuidados en América Latina y el Caribe.*

The distribution of paid and unpaid work in a couple typically starts diverging more with parenthood. This is a pattern common to all countries, including those supposedly characterised by more enshrined egalitarian attitudes and equal labour market outcomes. For new mothers there is a risk that a temporary arrangement within the couple could become permanent through custom and practice. Much about the actual outcome will depend upon parents' attitudes and their relative labour income (Schober, 2011[64]; Sanchez and Thomson, 1997[65]).

In Chile, almost half of all couples with children under 15 years old include one parent who works full-time and the other who does not work for pay (Table 1.1). This share is far higher than across the 29 OECD countries for which the information is available, which, conversely, have much higher shares of couples with both parents working full-time, or one parent working full-time and the other part-time. The reasons behind this imbalance can be practical, if, for example, a mother were still breast-feeding or had children who cannot benefit from proper care services. In addition, the outbreak of the COIVID-19 pandemic has shown that the capacity of parents to find suitable solutions to better balance domestic and work related responsibilities also reflects the access to flexible working hours, or options to work remotely. However, these practical considerations have to be weighted with the role played by cultural attitudes, according to which care and homework duties are 'women's prerogatives'. Financial considerations often compound the influence of these factors even further, particularly the belief that the woman partner would earn less than the man would. Even single mothers frequently do not work for pay in Chile, as revealed by the fact that approximately one-third of single parents, most of whom are women, do not work. The COVID-19 crisis has strongly re-shuffled men and women's paid and unpaid work, in ways that Section 3 below discusses in detail.

Table 1.1. In almost one half of families with children in Chile, one partner does not work

	Employment patterns in couples with at least one child aged 0-14 (% distribution)				
	Both partners full-time	One partner full-time, one partner part-time	One partner full-time, one partner not working	Both partners not working	Other
Chile	32.1	10.8	48.2	3.3	5.7
Costa Rica	26.9	15.6	50.4	1.9	5.2
Peru	35.2	32	22.8	1.2	8.7
OECD-29 average	41.9	16.6	30.8	5.3	5.4
	Single parents with at least one child aged 0-14 by employment status (%)				
	Working full-time	Working part-time	Working – no information on hours	Not working	
Costa Rica	49.5	19.8		30.7	
Chile	51.3	15.5	0.4	32.8	
Peru	64.7	24.8		10.5	
OECD-29 average	50.5	14.5	0.7	34.3	

Note: Data for Peru is for 2018, for Costa Rica to 2014, for Chile 2013 and the OECD for the latest available year in 2012-13. For Chile, the distinction between part-time and full-time work is based on actual hours worked in the main job during the survey reference week, rather than usual weekly working hours. For Peru, working hours were imputed when responses were missing.

Source: OECD (n.d.[43]), "LMF2.2 Patterns of employment and the distribution of working hours for couples with children" and "LMF2.3 Patterns of employment and the distribution of working hours for single parents ", *OECD Family Database*, http://www.oecd.org/social/family/database.htm; and own estimations based on the INE (2019[44]), *Encuesta Nacional de Hogares*.

Stereotypes and attitudes to gender equality

Gender stereotypes can influence female employment in multiple ways. With regard to the supply of labour, they can lead women to shy away from actively looking for a job in the labour market, for example (Christiansen et al., 2016[66]). Worse still, this effect often appears compounded by the partner's attitude, if they share the same wary attitude or even believes that it is their right to inhibit their wife from actively looking for a paid job. Restrictive masculinities, such that 'real' men should be the breadwinner and out-earn women, can contribute to the exclusion of women from high-status and highly paid positions (OECD, 2021[67]). In addition to affecting the supply of female labour, attitudes about gender roles can influence the demand for female labour. For example, those employers who believe that certain jobs should go to men rather than women, will less likely employ women, or pay them the same wage, if they hire them. There is evidence that the gender pay gap tends to be larger in countries in which a high proportion of men believe that scarce jobs should go to men first (Fortin, 2005[68]).

However, an analysis of Ecuador, Mexico and Peru explores whether differences in the total time worked by women and men can be explained by differences in gendered social norms (Campaña, Giménez-Nadal and Molina, 2018[69]). The findings corroborate the view that countries with more egalitarian attitudes have lower gaps in the total work burdens between men and women. In addition, a change in patterns driven by an expansion of the opportunities for women to find a paid job will likely entail positive feedback effects on gender attitudes, leading attitudes to improve over time (Seguino, 2007[70]).

The evidence available suggests that the traditional male breadwinner *vis-a-vis* female homeworker divide is still common in Chile, possibly more so than in other OECD countries, which contributes to perpetuate existing attitudes and stereotypes. Unfortunately, the situation may have worsened even further in the aftermath of COVID-19 (see, Section 3 below). For several years, the World Value Survey has conducted international comparative analyses by inviting feedbacks on a selection of proxies for traditional norms, such as the following, for example:

- The 'right' of women to participate in the labour market and education ("When jobs are scarce, men should have more right to a job than women" and "A university education is more important for a boy than a girl");
- The existence of a gender bias in political leadership ("On the whole, men make better political leaders than women"); and
- The compatibility of being a mother with a working life ("When a mother works for pay, children suffer").

The share of people who agree with the above traditional norms has declined over time in many countries (Seguino, 2007[70]). However, Chile stands out in the international comparison in a number of conservative beliefs (Figure 1.14). In particular, a lot more men than women continue to believe that men have more rights to participate in the labour market, are better political leaders and that access to university is more important for boys in Chile than it is for girls. In addition to being wide, these gaps are several percentage points higher than observed for the average of Latin American and OECD countries. At the same time, the difference in the prevalence of conservative attitudes between older and younger Chileans is also particularly pronounced, with younger people having a more egalitarian attitude than older people do (OECD, 2016[71]).

Figure 1.14. In Chile the share of men and women with traditional views on women's role in economic life varies more than elsewhere

Share of respondents to 2017-20 World Values Survey who (strongly) agree with the statement

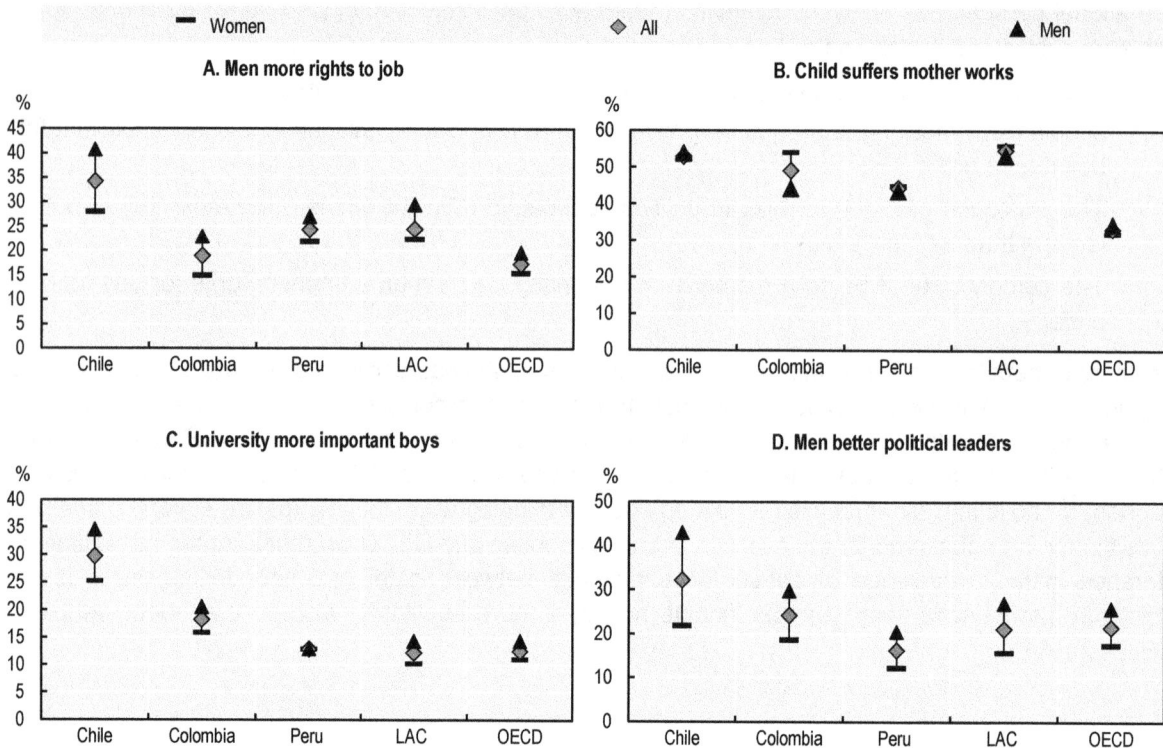

Note: The statements respondents are asked about are: "When jobs are scarce, men should have more right to a job than women."; If a woman earns more money than her husband, it's almost certain to cause problems."; "When a mother works for pay, the children suffer."; "A university education is more important for a boy than a girl."; "On the whole, men make better political leaders than women do.". The Latin American average is based on Argentina, Brazil, Chile, Colombia, Ecuador, Mexico, Peru and Uruguay. The OECD (15) average is based on Australia, Chile, Colombia, Germany, Japan, South Korea, Mexico, the Netherlands, New Zealand, Poland, Slovenia, Spain, Sweden, Turkey and the United States.
Source: Haerpfer et al. (2020[72]), *World Values Survey: Round 7 – Country-Pooled Datafile.*

Institutions and laws

Institutions and laws can have an important effect on the employment outcomes of women. Analysis across a range of developing and emerging economies suggests that factors such as equality under the law, equal inheritance and recognition of the right for women to be head of the household, are associated with a decline in the gender gap in labour force participation of around 4.6 percentage points (Gonzales et al., 2015[73]).

The OECD Development Centre's Social Institutions and Gender Index (SIGI), collects systematic measurement indicators of discrimination against women in social institutions for 180 countries. By taking into account laws, social norms and practices, the SIGI captures the underlying drivers of gender inequality with the aim to provide the data necessary for transformative policy change. The latest edition of the SIGI (OECD, 2020[61]) rates the overall level of gender discrimination in Chile as medium (Table 1.2). In this context, it portrays a number of contrasting results, with the presence of few restrictions to the civil liberties and physical integrity of women, co-existing with persistently high levels of discrimination in the family, and restricted access to productive and financial resources. The World Bank's *Women, Business and the Law* index score of Chile was 80 out of 100, below the OECD and Latin American averages (Table 1.3).

One important issue for concerns in Chile relates to the regulation of marital property rights. Although in principle couples can choose between three different regimes when they get married, more than 80% opt for the default option, which is the most restrictive and disadvantageous to women since it foresees that the husband administers the marital property (OECD, 2020[61]). This regime, which is only present in a handful of other countries, implies that it is difficult for married women to start or close a business without the consent of the husband because of lack of collateral. Accordingly, female entrepreneurs a pay higher interest rates. A reform proposal has been under discussion in Congress for the past eight years.

Table 1.2. The SIGI survey shows that discriminatory institutional practices are more common in Chile than elsewhere in Latin America

	SIGI		Discrimination in the family		Restricted physical integrity		Restricted access to productive and financial resources		Restricted civil liberties	
	Score	Cat.	Score	Cat.	Score	Cat.	Score	Cat.	Score	Cat.
Colombia	15	Very low	9.6	Very low	14.9	Low	14.5	Low	20.6	Low
Peru	24.5	Low	47.7	Medium	26.6	Medium	5.5	Very low	12.9	Low
Costa Rica	27.9	Low	45.7	Medium	24.8	Low	27.5	Medium	10.5	Low
Chile	36.1	Medium	36.4	Medium	18.8	Low	64.8	High	16.6	Low
Latin America	25.4		31.2		21.8		22.9		20.2	
OECD	17.2		25.1		12.6		13.4		17.3	

Note: The Latin American and OECD averages are unweighted means. The Latin American and the Caribbean average of the SIGI is based on Bolivia, Brazil, Colombia, Chile, Costa Rica, the Dominican Republic, Ecuador, El Salvador, Haiti, Guatemala, Jamaica, Honduras, Mexico, Nicaragua, Paraguay, Peru, Trinidad and Tobago and Uruguay. The discrimination in the family indicator is, in addition, based on Antigua and Barbuda, Bahamas, Barbados, Belise, Cuba, Dominica, Grenada, Guyana, Argentina, Panama and Venezuela (the latter three also for the productive and financial resources and civil liberties dimensions).
Source: OECD (2020[61]), *Social Institutions and Gender Index: Regional Report on Latin America and the Caribbean.*

Table 1.3. The Women, Business and the Law index shows that Chile underperforms in various dimensions

	WBL INDEX	Mobility	Workplace	Pay	Marriage	Parenthood	Entrepreneurship	Assets	Pension
Chile	77.5	100	75	75	60	100	75	60	75
Colombia	81.9	100	100	50	100	80	75	100	50
Costa Rica	80.0	100	100	25	100	40	75	100	100
Peru	95.0	100	100	100	80	80	100	100	100
LAC	80.4	94.4	82.4	70.4	85.9	51.9	83.3	97.0	77.8
OECD	93.7	100.0	97.9	88.2	94.4	88.9	94.4	98.9	86.8

Note: The LAC and OECD averages are unweighted. For the index, 35 questions are scored across the eight indicators based on laws and regulations that were in force at the time of the development of the index. Overall scores were calculated by taking the average of each indicator, with 100 representing the highest possible score.
Source: World Bank (2020[74]), *Women, Business and the Law data 1970-2020.*

Violence

Women can experience violence from their current and former partners or other family members but also in the office, at school and university, on public transport and in the streets. The victims of harassment, sexual and physical abuse and rape suffer physically and mentally (Ministerio del Interior y Seguridad Publica, 2020[75]). On top of these consequences, violence in domestic and public spaces, at school and at work undermines the educational and economic opportunities of the women who suffer it (ILO, 2018[76]).

In the first place, this reflects the fact that they are more frequently absent from school or the workplace to avoid dangerous situations, which directly affects academic achievements, productivity at work and well-being (ECLAC, 2016[77]). A high percentage of girls who experience a traumatic episode of this nature decide to change schools or leave the educational system altogether (OCAC, 2020[78]). For women who end up quitting their job, this decision has consequent impacts on careers and job opportunities (ILO, 2018[76]). The forced decision to restrict movements also limits the enjoyment of life (OCAC, 2020[78]).

In Chile, women are far more likely to experience harassment than men are. According to a recent survey by the Observatory Against Harassment (OCAC), 64% of women and 26% of men indicated that they had experienced non-verbal, physical or another type of harassment (OCAC, 2020[78]). More specifically:

- The share of women who declare to have experienced harassment in public spaces is twice as high as the share of men who do. Not only do women experience this situation more frequently, they also experience it at a younger age. Half of the affected stated that, as a result, they changed their behaviour in some way, such as changing itinerary, mode of transport, or asking a man to accompany them.

- In the workplace, three out of ten women have suffered non-verbal harassment; two out of ten have experienced both verbal harassment and physical harassment. In most cases, the perpetrator of the harassment or assault is either a co-worker (45%) or a manager (36%). Nearly a quarter of women who experienced sexual harassment at work quit the job, and around 40% avoided certain areas.

- At school or university, almost a third each have experienced non-verbal and physical harassment and a sixth verbal harassment. Two thirds of the perpetrators are fellow students, and slightly more than a fifth, teachers or professors. Approximately one in four women who were victims of harassment while studying left common places and/or situations with their aggressor and one in ten consulted a psychiatrist or psychologist.

- Faced with situations of violence, women are almost five times more likely to drop out of their studies than men (9.3% and 1.9%, respectively). Moreover, evidence from a 2015/16 study among female university students at the University of Chile shows that, while initially only 6.5% expressed having been a victim of sexual harassment within the university's premises, the share more than doubles to 14.7% when asked about specific experiences (Universidad de Chile, 2019[79]).

The intolerance of violence against women has increased during the past years in Chile, as part of a broad pattern whereby Chileans feel increasingly concerned by all forms of violence, whether associated with crimes, intolerance or discrimination. However, there are also signs that the social perception of violence continues to vary within the population, as revealed by the fact that around 10% of the Chileans continue to minimise the relevance of the problem (Pontificia Universidad Católica de Chile, 2020[80]). Many young women, particularly from low-income households, still believe that the violence they suffer is not worth reporting to the authorities on the ground that it is not serious enough, (CEAD, 2020[81]). At the same time, the study among female university students at the University of Chile also noted that many victims of sexual harassment do not report it because of shame or fear of reprisal (Universidad de Chile, 2019[79]). Taken together, these findings suggest that raising awareness of the relevance of violence against women is a long-standing challenge that cuts across different social groups and levels of education. During the COVID-19 pandemic, strict lockdown conditions have exacerbated this situation even further, amid growing risks of violence, exploitation and abuse against women (Section 3).

Care and physical infrastructure

A further factor that can contribute to differences in economic outcomes between men and women is the physical and social infrastructure and, related to this, the availability of labour-saving household technology. On the one hand, the availability of reliable and affordable facilities, such as local buses and trains, child and elder care facilities, along with electricity and running water, affect how many hours adult household members need to spend on commuting, looking after children, cooking and cleaning and the hours that they can devote to paid work. On the other hand, access to public infrastructure affects how safe people feel and hence their perception about what activities they can pursue. For example, if girls and women have to cross poorly lit areas to get to school or to work, or if sexual harassment is common on public transport, they will avoid going out when it is dark or taking the bus. Insecurity limits the range of economic and leisure options open to women.

The availability of infrastructure varies strongly by geographic area, as well as by households' income levels. Well-off households are generally more likely to live in areas where different types of infrastructure are available and typically of higher quality. Moreover, even if a certain infrastructure is not available in a particular area, richer people will likely compensate more easily for this absence. For example, instead of using public transport, high-income women can drive a car; and instead of sending their children to a public day care centre, they can hire a nanny or pay for a private day care centre.

Access to affordable and quality formal or informal childcare is a key factor in supporting the participation of women in the labour market (Mateo Díaz and Rodriguez-Chamussy, 2016[82]). In Chile, four in five pre-school children aged three to five years enrol in early childhood education and care (Figure 1.15). However, only one in five children under the age of three attends early childhood care, considerably below the OECD average. This lengthens the time that women spend in early childcare.

In addition to childcare, many women also assist their elderly relatives at home, with women in their middle age shouldering much of this extra burden. Compared to childcare, the care of the elderly is at times even more difficult to plan, which makes the combination between care and work activities more cumbersome (Laczko and Noden, n.d.[83]). Different researchers have come to different conclusions as to whether the proximity to day care facilities, with suitable opening hours, increases female labour force participation. According to Contreras, Puentes and Bravo (2012[84]), the effect is positive; while Medrano (2009[85]) and Encina and Martinez (2009[86]) find no effect. The current state of the Chilean care system and options as to how to strengthen it are discussed in detail in the following section on the policies to support more equal sharing of paid and unpaid work.

Figure 1.15. One in five pre-school children are not in early childhood education in Chile

Percentage of children enrolled in early childhood education and care services or in primary education, by age group, 2017 or most recent

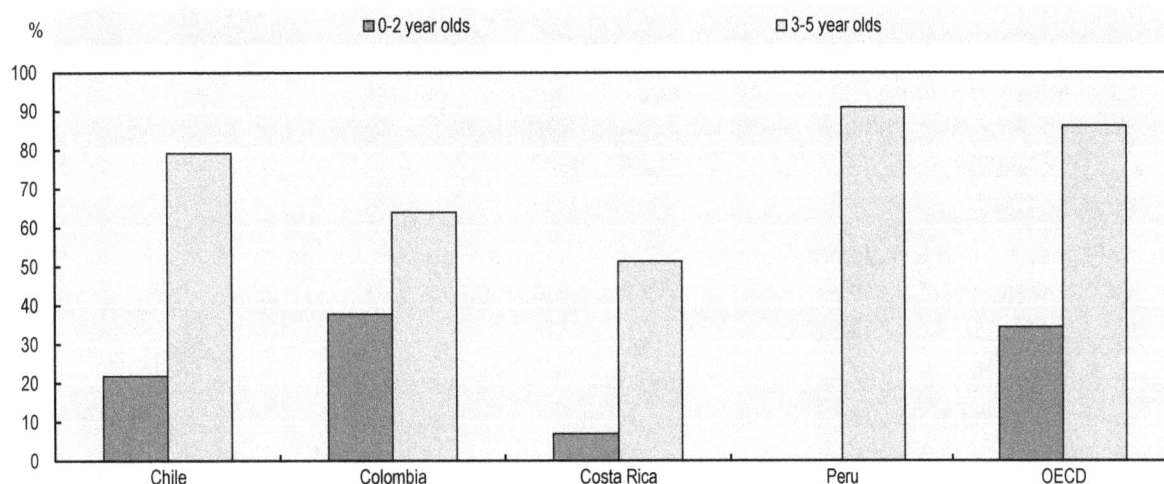

Note: The OECD average does not include Canada. Peru refers to 2018.
Source: OECD (n.d.[43]), "Formal care and education for very young children – PF3.2 Enrolment in childcare and pre-school", *OECD Family Database*, http://www.oecd.org/els/family/database.htm and MINEDU (2019[87]), "Tasa neta de asistencia, educación inicial (% de población con edades 3-5)", *Estadística de la Calidad Educativa.*

Long and onerous commutes negatively affect the well-being and economic opportunities of men and women alike. However, it is important to underline that transport needs may differ on average between women and men. Across many countries, men tend to spend more time commuting to and from work. Women, instead, more frequently make short or multi-stop trips that consist for example in dropping a child at school before work and stopping by the market on the way home from work. They are also more likely to walk and take public transport and less likely to drive (Duchène, 2011[88]). These patterns are also common across all Latin American cities (Dominguez Gonzalez et al., 2020[89]). In many large cities, the transport system is often set up to ferry passengers from the periphery to the centre, which puts the women who need to move between different areas of the outskirts at a disadvantage.

Even if transport options are available, women may be reluctant to take them if they are afraid of being robbed, sexually harassed or otherwise attacked. A 2014 survey of 15 of the 20 largest capitals around the world, found that women in Latin American cities feel most unsafe (in particular in Bogota, followed by Mexico City and Lima) (Boros, 2014[90]). In Santiago, a higher share of women than men use public transport (Granada et al., 2019[91]) and they generally feel less safe than men do. Women who can afford switching to other forms of transport, such as their own cars or cabs, choose the alternative option. Others have to adapt the hours during which they use transport, or avoid traveling alone (Allen et al., 2018[92]). Poorer households also less frequently live close to public infrastructures, such as bus stops or train stations (90.1% in the first income quintile, compared to 96.7% in the fifth), educational institutions (86.5% compared to 95.0%) and health centres (78.5% compared to 88.9%). This means that they frequently have to travel longer distances to access transportation, education and health services (Observatorio Social, 2018[93]).

Furthermore, the efforts required to maintaining a household in good condition, and hence the hours available for other activities, depends upon the access to electricity and labour-saving technology. Appliances such as the washing machine have massively reduced the physical and time effort needed to wash clothes, clean the home and cook. The timesaving effects of household appliances is so important that some economists believe that they have changed the world more than the internet (Chang, 2012[94]). In Chile, 99.7% of households had access to electricity in 2018, but in rural areas, 1.4% still were not on the electricity grid (World Bank, n.d.[95]; Red de Pobreza Energética, n.d.[96]).

References

Allen, H. et al. (2018), *Ella se mueve segura (ESMS) – A study on women's personal safety in public transport in three Latin American cities*, CAF and FIA Foundation, https://scioteca.caf.com/bitstream/handle/123456789/1407/Ella%20se%20mueve%20segura%20%E2%80%93%20A%20study%20on%20womens%20personal%20safety.pdf?sequence=5&isAllowed=y. [92]

Arceo-Gomez, E. and R. Campos-Vazquez (2014), "Teenage Pregnancy in Mexico: Evolution and Consequences", *Latin American Journal of Economics*, Vol. 51/1, http://dx.doi.org/10.7764/LAJE.51.1.109. [25]

Boros, C. (2014), *EXCLUSIVE-POLL: Latin American cities have most dangerous transport for women, NYC best*, Reuters, London, https://uk.reuters.com/article/women-poll/exclusive-poll-latin-american-cities-have-most-dangerous-transport-for-women-nyc-best-idUKL6N0S32MQ20141029. [90]

Campaña, J., J. Giménez-Nadal and J. Molina (2018), "Gender Norms and the Gendered Distribution of Total Work in Latin American Households", *Feminist Economics*, doi: 10.1080/13545701.2017.1390320, pp. 35-62, http://dx.doi.org/10.1080/13545701.2017.1390320. [69]

CEAD (2020), *Informe de Resultados IV Encuesta de Violencia contra la Mujer en el Ámbito de Violencia Intrafamiliar y en Otros Espacios (ENVIF-VCM)*, http://cead.spd.gov.cl/centro-de-documentacion/. [81]

Chang, H. (2012), *23 things they don't tell you about capitalism*, Bloomsbury Publishing, London. [94]

Christiansen, L. et al. (2016), "Individual Choice or Policies? Drivers of Female Employment in Europe", *IMF Working Paper*, No. 16/49. [66]

Comunidad Mujer (2020), *Cuanto aportamos al PIB?*, https://www.comunidadmujer.cl/biblioteca-publicaciones/wp-content/uploads/2020/03/Cuánto-aportamos-al-PIB.-Primer-Estudio-de-Valoración-Económica-del-Trabajo-Doméstico-y-de-Cuidado.pdf (accessed on 22 March 2021). [17]

CONICYT (2018), *Reporte de participacion femenina periodo 2009-2018*, https://www.conicyt.cl/wp-content/uploads/2015/03/REPORTE-DE-GENERO-2018-_VF.pdf. [53]

Connolly, S. and M. Gregory (2008), "Moving Down: Women's Part-Time Work and Occupational Change in Britain 1991–2001*", *The Economic Journal*, doi: 10.1111/j.1468-0297.2007.02116.x, pp. F52-F76, http://dx.doi.org/10.1111/j.1468-0297.2007.02116.x. [11]

Conti, G., J. Heckman and S. Urzua (2010), "The Education-Health Gradient", *American Economic Review*, Vol. 100/2, pp. 234-238, http://dx.doi.org/10.1257/aer.100.2.234. [2]

Contreras, D., E. Puentes and D. Bravo (2012), "Female Labor Supply and Child Care Supply in Chile", *Department of Economics Working Paper*, No. 340, University of Chile, Santiago, https://ideas.repec.org/p/udc/wpaper/wp370.html. [84]

Dávila-Cervantes, C. and M. Agudelo-Botero (2019), "Health inequalities in Latin America: persistent gaps in life expectancy", *The Lancet Planetary Health*, doi: 10.1016/S2542-5196(19)30244-X, pp. e492-e493, http://dx.doi.org/10.1016/S2542-5196(19)30244-X. [3]

Dominguez Gonzalez, K. et al. (2020), *Why does she move? A Study of Women's Mobility in Latin American Cities*, World Bank, Washington, D.C., http://documents.worldbank.org/curated/en/276931583534671806/pdf/Why-Does-She-Move-A-Study-of-Womens-Mobility-in-Latin-American-Cities.pdf. [89]

Dougherty, C. (2005), "Why Are the Returns to Schooling Higher for Women than for Men?", *The Journal of Human Resources*, Vol. 40/4, pp. 969-988, http://www.jstor.org/stable/4129547. [7]

Duchène, C. (2011), "Gender and Transport", *Discussion Paper*, No. 11, International Transport Forum, Paris. [88]

ECLAC (2019), *Poder legislativo: porcentaje de mujeres en el órgano legislativo nacional: Cámara baja o única*, https://oig.cepal.org/es/indicadores/poder-legislativo-porcentaje-mujeres-organo-legislativo-nacional-camara-baja-o-unica (accessed on October 2020). [58]

ECLAC (2018), *Los cuidados en América Latina y el Caribe*, Economic Commission for Latin America and the Caribbean, Santiago de Chile. [63]

ECLAC (2017), *Reproduccion en la adolescencia en Chile: la desigualdad continua y urgen politicas activas*, https://diprece.minsal.cl/wrdprss_minsal/wp-content/uploads/2017/04/Estudio-CEPAL-elaborado-en-el-marco-del-Acuerdo-que-tiene-con-UNFPA.pdf. [33]

ECLAC (2016), *Otras formas de violencia contra la mujer*, https://repositorio.cepal.org/bitstream/handle/11362/40754/4/S1601170_es.pdf. [77]

Encina, J. and C. Martínez (2009), "Efecto de una mayor cobertura de salas cuna en la participación laboral femenina: evidencia de Chile", *Department of Economics Working Paper*, No. 303, University of Chile, Santiago, https://ideas.repec.org/p/udc/wpaper/wp303.html. [86]

Ferrant, G., L. Pesando and K. Nowacka (2014), "Unpaid Care Work: The missing link in the analysis of gender gaps in labour outcomes", OECD Development Centre, Paris, http://www.oecd.org/dev/development-gender/unpaid_care_work.pdf. [10]

Ferrant, G. and A. Thim (2019), "Measuring Women's Economic Empowerment: Time Use Data and Gender Inequality", *OECD Development Policy Papers*, No. 16, OECD Publishing, https://doi.org/10.1787/02e538fc-en. [16]

Fortin, N. (2005), "Gender Role Attitudes and the Labour-market Outcomes of Women across OECD Countries", *Oxford Review of Economic Policy*, Vol. 21/3, pp. 416-438, http://dx.doi.org/10.1093/oxrep/gri024. [68]

Gonzales, C. et al. (2015), "Fair Play: More Equal Laws Boost Female Labor Force Participation", *IMF Staff Discussion Paper*, No. 15/02, International Monetary Fund, Washington, D.C. [73]

Granada, I. et al. (2019), *Género y Transporte: Santiago*, Interamerican Development Bank, Washington, D.C. [91]

Haerpfer, C. et al. (2020), *World Values Survey: Round Seven - Country-Pooled Datafile*. [72]

IDB (2018), *Women at the Forefront of Economic Prosperity in the 21st Century*, https://publications.iadb.org/publications/english/document/Women-at-the-Forefront-of-Economic-Prosperity-in-the-21st-Century.pdf. [55]

ILO (2018), *Acabar con la violencia y el acoso contra las mujeres y los hombres en el mundo del trabajo*, https://www.ilo.org/wcmsp5/groups/public/---ed_norm/---relconf/documents/meetingdocument/wcms_554100.pdf. [76]

ILO (2018), *Global Wage Report 2018/19: What lies behind gender pay gaps*, International Labour Office, Geneva, https://www.ilo.org/wcmsp5/groups/public/---dgreports/---dcomm/---publ/documents/publication/wcms_650553.pdf. [50]

ILO (n.d.), *ILOSTAT*, https://ilostat.ilo.org/ (accessed on 29 April 2020). [42]

ILO, MINTRAB and MINDESARROLLO (2013), *Magnitud y características del trabajo infantil en Chile - Informe 2013*, Organización Internacional del Trabajo, Programa Internacional para la Erradicación del Trabajo Infantil (IPEC), Ministerio del Trabajo y Previsión Social y Ministerio de Desarrollo Social de Ch, http://white.lim.ilo.org/ipec/documentos/oit_chile_2013.pdf. [22]

INE (2019), *Encuesta Nacional de Hogares*, Instituto Nacional de Estadística e InformáticaA, Lima, https://webinei.inei.gob.pe/anda_inei/index.php/catalog/613/. [44]

Jonas, N. and W. Thorn (2018), "Literacy skills and family configurations", *OECD Education Working Papers*, No. 192, OECD Publishing, Paris, https://dx.doi.org/10.1787/509d788a-en. [28]

Kahn, S. and D. Ginther (2018), "Women and Science, Technology, Engineering, and Mathematics (STEM): Are Differences in Education and Careers Due to Stereotypes, Interests, or Family?", in Averett, S., L. Argys and S. Hoffman (eds.), *The Oxford Handbook of Women and the Economy*, Oxford University Press, Oxford, http://dx.doi.org/10.1093/oxfordhb/9780190628963.013.13. [38]

Laczko, F. and S. Noden (n.d.), "Combining paid work with eldercare: the implications for social policy", *Health and Social Care*, Vol. 1, pp. 81-89, https://onlinelibrary.wiley.com/doi/pdf/10.1111/j.1365-2524.1993.tb00200.x. [83]

MacDonald, M., S. Phipps and L. Lethbridge (2005), "Taking Its Toll: The Influence of Paid and Unpaid Work on Women's Well-Being", *Feminist Economics*, doi: 10.1080/1354570042000332597, pp. 63-94, http://dx.doi.org/10.1080/1354570042000332597. [12]

Mandakovic, V. et al. (2017), *Mujeres y actividad emprendedora en Chile 2017*, Universidad del Desarrollo, Santiago. [45]

Marcus, R. and E. Page (2016), *Girls' Learning and Empowerment - The Role of School Environments*, United Nations Girls' Education Initiative, http://www.ungei.org/Policy_Brief_-_School_Environments-v2.pdf. [9]

Mateo Díaz, M. and L. Rodriguez-Chamussy (2016), *Cashing in on Education - Women, Childcare, and Prosperity in Latin America and the Caribbean*, International Bank for Reconstruction and Development / The World Bank, Washington, D.C. [82]

Medrano, P. (2009), "Public Day Care and Female Labor Force Participation: Evidence from Chile", *Department of Economics Working Paper*, No. 306, University of Chile, Santiago, http://econ.uchile.cl/uploads/publicacion/25d848f1-0435-4691-9623-b20cff7a36aa.pdf. [85]

Mincer, J. (1984), "Human capital and economic growth", *Economics of Education Review*, Vol. 3/3, pp. 195-205, https://doi.org/10.1016/0272-7757(84)90032-3. [4]

MINDES (2018), "Equidad de Género: Sintesis de Resultados CASEN 2017", http://observatorio.ministeriodesarrollosocial.gob.cl/casen-multidimensional/casen/docs/CASEN_2017_EQUIDAD_DE_GENERO.pdf. [51]

MINEDU (2019), *Estadistica de la Calidad Educativa*, http://escale.minedu.gob.pe/ueetendencias2016 (accessed on 26 May 2020). [87]

MINEDUC (2020), *Medicion de la exclusion escolar en Chile*, https://centroestudios.mineduc.cl/wp-content/uploads/sites/100/2020/04/DOCUMENTO-DE-TRABAJO-20_2020_f01.pdf (accessed on 3 October 2020). [21]

Ministerio de Economia Fomento y Turismo (2020), *Boletín EME-6: Género y Microemprendimiento*, https://www.economia.gob.cl/2020/12/31/boletin-eme-6-genero-y-microemprendimiento.htm (accessed on 22 March 2021). [47]

Ministerio de Economía Fomento y Turismo (2017), *Informe de resultados: Empresas en Chile*, Ministerio de Economía, Fomento y Turismo. [48]

Ministerio del Interior y Seguridad Publica (2020), *IV Encuesta de Violencia contra la Mujer en el Ambito de Violencia Intrafamiliar y en Otros Espacios (ENVIF-VCM) Resultados Pais*, http://cead.spd.gov.cl/wp-content/uploads/file-manager/Presentaci%C3%B3n%20de%20Resultados%20IV%20ENVIF-VCM.pdf (accessed on 22 March 2021). [75]

MINSAL (2013), *Situacion actual del embarazo adolescente en Chile*, Ministerio del Salud, Santiago, https://www.minsal.cl/portal/url/item/c908a2010f2e7dafe040010164010db3.pdf. [31]

Modrego, F., D. Paredes and G. Romaní (2017), "Individual and place-based drivers of self-employment in Chile", *Small Business Economics*, Vol. 49/2, pp. 469-492, http://dx.doi.org/10.1007/s11187-017-9841-2. [46]

Montenegro, C. and H. Patrinos (2014), "Comparable estimates of returns to schooling around the world", *Policy Research Working Paper*, No. 7020, World Bank, Washington, D.C., http://documents.worldbank.org/curated/en/830831468147839247/Comparable-estimates-of-returns-to-schooling-around-the-world. [6]

NEAL, S. (2018), *The impact of young maternal age at birth on neonatal mortality: Evidence from 45 low and middle income countries*, https://www.ncbi.nlm.nih.gov/pmc/articles/PMC5965834/ (accessed on 19 March 2021). [35]

Nollenberger, N., N. Rodríguez-Planas and A. Sevilla (2016), "The Math Gender Gap: The Role of Culture", *American Economic Review*, Vol. 106/5, pp. 257-261, http://dx.doi.org/10.1257/aer.p20161121. [39]

Observatorio Social (2018), *CASEN 2017 Síntesis de Resultados Vivienda y Entorno*, Ministerio de Desarrollo Social, Santiago, http://observatorio.ministeriodesarrollosocial.gob.cl/casen-multidimensional/casen/docs/Resultados_vivienda_casen_2017.pdf. [93]

Observatorio Social (2018), *Encuesta CASEN 2017 - Educación*, Ministerio de Desarrollo Social, Santiago, http://observatorio.ministeriodesarrollosocial.gob.cl/casen-multidimensional/casen/docs/Educacion_casen_2017.xlsx. [19]

Observatorio Social (2017), *Equidad de Gnéero: Indice de Resultados*, http://observatorio.ministeriodesarrollosocial.gob.cl/casen-multidimensional/casen/docs/CASEN_2017_EQUIDAD_DE_GENERO.pdf. [34]

OCAC (2020), *Radiografia del acoso sexual en Chile: Primera encuesta nacional sobre acoso sexual callejero, laboral, en*, https://www.ocac.cl/wp-content/uploads/2020/07/Informe-encuesta-OCAC-2020.-Radiograf%C3%ADa-del-acoso-sexual-en-Chile.pdf. [78]

OECD (2021), *Man Enough? Measuring Masculine Norms to Promote Women's Empowerment*, Social Institutions and Gender Index, OECD Publishing, Paris, https://dx.doi.org/10.1787/6ffd1936-en. [67]

OECD (2020), *Education at a Glance 2020: OECD Indicators*, OECD Publishing, Paris, https://dx.doi.org/10.1787/69096873-en. [60]

OECD (2020), *SIGI 2020 Regional Report for Latin America and the Caribbean*, Social Institutions and Gender Index, OECD Publishing, Paris, https://doi.org/10.1787/cb7d45d1-en. [61]

OECD (2019), *Education at a Glance 2019: OECD Indicators*, OECD Publishing, Paris, https://doi.org/10.1787/f8d7880d-en. [1]

OECD (2019), *Investing in Youth: Peru*, Investing in Youth, OECD Publishing, Paris, https://dx.doi.org/10.1787/9789264305823-en. [59]

OECD (2019), *PISA 2018 Results (Volume II): Where All Students Can Succeed*, PISA, OECD Publishing, Paris, https://dx.doi.org/10.1787/b5fd1b8f-en. [37]

OECD (2019), *Skills Matter: Additional Results from the Survey of Adult Skills*, OECD Skills Studies, OECD Publishing, Paris, https://dx.doi.org/10.1787/1f029d8f-en. [20]

OECD (2018), *OECD.Stat*, http://dotstat.oecd.org/?lang=en. [40]

OECD (2018), "Teenage parenthood: How does it relate to proficiency in literacy?", *Adult Skills in Focus*, No. 9, OECD Publishing, Paris, https://dx.doi.org/10.1787/de7859a0-en. [27]

OECD (2017), *OECD Family Database - Key characteristics of parental leave systems*, OECD Publishing, Paris, http://www.oecd.org/els/soc/PF2_1_Parental_leave_systems.pdf. [62]

OECD (2017), *Women in politics: Women parlamentarians*, https://data.oecd.org/inequality/women-in-politics.htm. [57]

OECD (2016), *Gender Equality in the Pacific Alliance: Promoting Women's Economic Empowerment*, OECD Publishing, Paris, https://dx.doi.org/10.1787/9789264262959-en. [71]

OECD (2016), *Improving Women's Access to Leadership: What Works?*, OECD, Paris, https://www.oecd.org/about/secretary-general/improving-womens-access-to-leadership-what-works.htm. [54]

OECD (2016), *Skills Matter: Further Results from the Survey of Adult Skills*, OECD Skills Studies, OECD Publishing, Paris, https://dx.doi.org/10.1787/9789264258051-en. [36]

OECD (n.d.), *Employment database*, https://www.oecd.org/employment/labour-stats/onlineoecdemploymentdatabase.htm (accessed on 29 April 2020). [41]

OECD (n.d.), *LFS - Decile ratios of gross earnings*, https://stats.oecd.org/Index.aspx?QueryId=64193 (accessed on 29 April 2020). [49]

OECD (n.d.), *OECD Family Database*, http://www.oecd.org/social/family/database.htm. [43]

Ogolsky, B., R. Dennison and J. Monk (2014), "The Role of Couple Discrepancies in Cognitive and Behavioral Egalitarianism in Marital Quality", *Sex Roles*, Vol. 70/7, pp. 329-342, http://dx.doi.org/10.1007/s11199-014-0365-9. [14]

PAHO, UNFPA and UNICEF (2017), *Accelerating progress toward the reduction of adolescent pregnancy in Latin America and the Caribbean*, Pan American Health Organization / World Health Organization, Washington, D.C., https://iris.paho.org/bitstream/handle/10665.2/34493/9789275119761-eng.pdf?sequence=1&isAllowed=y&ua=1. [32]

PNUD (2020), *Nuevo Mapa del Poder y Género en Chile (1995-2018)*, https://www.cl.undp.org/content/chile/es/home/library/crisis_prevention_and_recovery/nuevo-mapa-del-poder-y-genero-en-chile--1995-2018-.html. [56]

Pontificia Universidad Católica de Chile (2020), *Encuesta Nacional Bicentenario*, https://encuestabicentenario.uc.cl/resultados/ (accessed on 27 July 2020). [80]

Post, D. (2011), "Primary school student employment and academic achievement in Chile, Colombia, Ecuador and Peru", *International Labour Review*, Vol. 150/3-4, pp. 255-278. [23]

Post, D. and S. Pong (2009), "The academic effects of after-school paid and unpaid work among 14-year-old students in TIMSS countries", *Compare: A Journal of Comparative and International Education*, doi: 10.1080/03057920802681804, pp. 799-818, http://dx.doi.org/10.1080/03057920802681804. [24]

Publimetro (2018), *Deserción escolar: 50% de las alumnas embarazadas no retoman posteriormente sus estudios*, https://www.publimetro.cl/cl/noticias/2018/03/05/desercion-escolar-50-las-alumnas-embarazadas-no-retoman-posteriormente-estudios.html (accessed on 3 October 2020). [26]

Red de Pobreza Energética (n.d.), *¿Qué es Pobreza Energética?*, http://redesvid.uchile.cl/pobreza-energetica/que-es-pobreza-energetica/ (accessed on 8 July 2020). [96]

Sanchez, L. and E. Thomson (1997), "Becoming Mothers and Fathers: Parenthood, Gender, and the Division of Labor", *Gender & Society*, doi: 10.1177/089124397011006003, pp. 747-772, http://dx.doi.org/10.1177/089124397011006003. [65]

Schober, P. (2011), "The Parenthood Effect on Gender Inequality: Explaining the Change in Paid and Domestic Work When British Couples Become Parents", *European Sociological Review*, Vol. 29/1, pp. 74-85, http://dx.doi.org/10.1093/esr/jcr041. [64]

Schultz, T. (1993), "Returns to Women's Education", in King, E. and M. Hill (eds.), *Women's Education in Developing Countries: Barriers, Benefits and Policies*, World Bank, Washington, D.C. [8]

Seguino, S. (2007), "Plus ça Change? Evidence on Global Trends in Gender Norms and Stereotypes", *Feminist Economics*, doi: 10.1080/13545700601184880, pp. 1-28, http://dx.doi.org/10.1080/13545700601184880. [70]

Sepúlveda, P. (2019), "Embarazo adolescente experimenta fuerte caída y registra la mitad de los casos que hace dos décadas", *La Tercera*, https://www.latercera.com/que-pasa/noticia/embarazo-adolescente-experimenta-fuerte-caida/695641/. [30]

Sigle-Rushton, W. (2010), "Men's Unpaid Work and Divorce: Reassessing Specialization and Trade in British Families", *Feminist Economics*, doi: 10.1080/13545700903448801, pp. 1-26, http://dx.doi.org/10.1080/13545700903448801. [13]

UNESCO (2015), *UNESCO Science Report*, https://en.unesco.org/unescosciencereport. [52]

UNESCO (2014), *Developing an education sector response to early and unintended pregnancy - Discussion document for a global consultation*, UNESCO, Paris, https://unesdoc.unesco.org/in/documentViewer.xhtml?v=2.1.196&id=p::usmarcdef_0000230510&file=/in/rest/annotationSVC/DownloadWatermarkedAttachment/attach_import_0cd6034f-c602-4e59-8e8d-e6b59c41d45d%3F_%3D230510eng.pdf&locale=en&multi=true&ark=/ark:/48223/p. [29]

UNESCO Institute for Statistics (n.d.), *UIS Database*, http://data.uis.unesco.org/ (accessed on 29 April 2020).   [18]

Universidad de Chile (2019), *Acoso en el campus: El acoso sexual en la Universidad de Chile*, https://direcciondegenero.uchile.cl/project/acosoenelcampus/.   [79]

WHO (2007), *Fatherhood and health outcomes in Europe*, World Health Organization , Copenhagen, http://www.euro.who.int/__data/assets/pdf_file/0017/69011/E91129.pdf.   [15]

Woodhall, M. (1973), "The economic returns to investment in women's education", *Higher Education*, Vol. 2/3, pp. 275-299, http://dx.doi.org/10.1007/BF00138806.   [5]

World Bank (2020), *Women, Business and the Law data for 1971-2020*, World Bank, Washington, D.C., https://wbl.worldbank.org/en/resources/data.   [74]

World Bank (n.d.), *World Development Indicators*, World Bank, Washington, D.C., https://data.worldbank.org.   [95]

Notes

[1] The gap in the average labour income between men and women in Chile in the fourth quarter of 2019 even amounted to 28.1%. The larger gap than reported by the OECD estimates can be explained on the one hand by the fact that men are over-represented among high-income earners (and this affects the mean but not the median) and that the OECD estimate is restricted to full-time workers.

2 A holistic policy framework for achieving a balanced sharing of paid and unpaid work

This chapter argues that achieving a better sharing of paid and unpaid responsibilities between men and women in Chile requires a comprehensive policy strategy and presents a holistic framework for its development using two policy axes. The first axis comprises the policies aimed at reducing the barriers that stand in the way of a more equitable division of time and responsibilities between men and women: Creating a more effective care system, expanding parental leave and reducing the transmission of gender stereotypes through the education system. The second axis includes the policies that aim to increase the participation of women in the labour market through ensuring that women's paid work pays more: Ensuring access to quality education for all, promoting women in non-traditional careers and leadership positions, supporting female entrepreneurship and fighting violence against women. The chapter reviews each area in detail and provides policy insights for possible improvements.

As discussed in Chapter 1, many societal, institutional and economic factors are behind the higher unpaid work burden of women and their less favourable economic outcomes. Policy changes, as well as shifts in attitudes, have already reduced gender gaps in the labour market and have practically eliminated them in basic education. Nonetheless, some girls in Chile continue to leave school prematurely, and many women steer away from better-paid scientific and technical careers, are less frequently employed in quality jobs, work more frequently in the informal sector and earn less money. Substantial welfare and income gains would accrue to both men and women by further reducing these gaps. A more equitable division of paid and unpaid work is therefore a worthwhile policy goal.

Given the variety of drivers of the current division of paid and unpaid work, Chile needs to implement a comprehensive policy strategy to move towards a more balanced sharing of activities between men and women. As a contribution to such a policy strategy, this chapter puts forward a holistic framework, building on two policy axes, namely the following:

- On the one hand, the policies aimed at reducing the barriers that currently stand in the way of a more equitable division of time and responsibilities between men and women, as distinguished from
- On the other hand, the policies that aim to increase the participation of women in the labour market through ensuring that women's paid work pays more.

The first policy axis focuses on reducing the burden of unpaid work that women have to carry out and the hurdles that make it difficult to share paid and unpaid and paid work more equally between genders. Key examples of the policy areas encompassed by this axis include the expansion of the public care system for both children and the elderly; introducing, or strengthening the regulations governing parental leaves and flexible work solutions; and promoting a gender-neutral approach at all levels of education.

The second policy axis spots light on the policies that contribute to reduce the gender gap in labour income, lessening, in turn, the incentive for women to spend long hours on unpaid work and freeing more hours for them to destine to paid work. Key examples of these policies include addressing any remaining barriers for all groups of girls to access quality education; the efforts to increase the share of women who work in the formal sector and have access to quality jobs; and fighting violence against women in public spaces and the workplace.

Figure 2.1 provides the diagrammatic illustration of the policy framework. The two policy axes are mutually reinforcing, in the sense that the interplay of positive policy changes across them will lead to significantly increasing the number of women who could and would like to work outside the home and that of men willing to take over caring and domestic tasks.

While not the only policies that could contribute to these changes, the specific areas addressed in this report emerged as the most relevant, in terms of both potential impact and feasibility, during a project's fact-finding mission to Santiago de Chile. The reminder of the chapter reviews each area in detail starting with an assessment of the challenges and existing policies. A set of policy insights will follow, building on the lesson from the international experience and the OECD knowledge of international practices.

Figure 2.1. A comprehensive policy framework for achieving a balanced sharing of paid and unpaid work in Chile

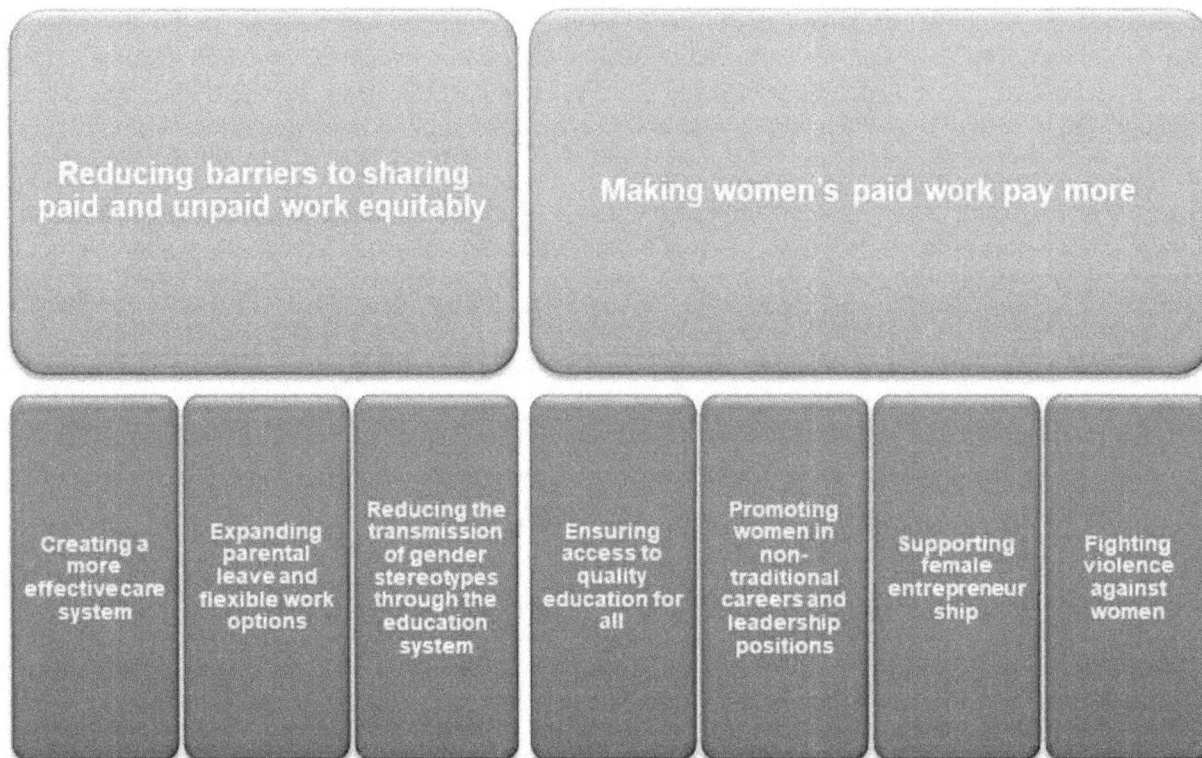

Reducing barriers to sharing paid and unpaid work equitably			Making women's paid work pay more			
Creating a more effective care system	Expanding parental leave and flexible work options	Reducing the transmission of gender stereotypes through the education system	Ensuring access to quality education for all	Promoting women in non-traditional careers and leadership positions	Supporting female entrepreneurship	Fighting violence against women

Reducing barriers to sharing paid and unpaid work equitably

Creating a more comprehensive care system

Caring activities for babies, children and disabled, ill or elderly adults make for an important share of unpaid domestic work. In the absence of a comprehensive national care system, the bulk of these activities falls primarily on women. On a typical day, women in Latin America spend in average 1.5 more time on care activities for members of their own household than men do (3.4 hours against 2.1 hours). In Chile the gap is wider, since women spend almost twice as much time on these activities (3.0 hours against 1.6 hours) (INE, 2016[1]). This is more than in Argentina (where women spend 1.1 more time on care activities than men do) and less than in Peru (where women spend 2.2 more time on these than men do) (ECLAC, 2018[2]). The availability of affordable public and private care services could contribute to a re-balancing of the care burden between genders, if complemented by broader efforts to shift attitudes, along with the policies to increase parental leaves and part-time work opportunities for men and women.

Although Chile has a mix of private and public provision of childcare, important challenges remain. According to Article 203 of the Labour Code, employers with more than 20 female workers must provide childcare assistance to children under the age of two. This obligation discourages employers from hiring women formally beyond the threshold and leaves women working for smaller or non-complying employers uncovered. The Ministry of Labour would like to replace the current 20 female workers threshold by a more universal system, accessible to all workers and poor women, financed through a 0.1% contribution on taxable salaries.

In addition to the above provision, the programme *Chile Crece Contigo* extends the coverage of childcare to poor working mothers and student mothers, who belong to the 60% most vulnerable women according to the needs-adjusted income information about their household contained in the Social Household Register. Another programme, named the *4 to 7 programme,* addresses the care gaps of school-aged children whose parents working hours are longer than school hours. A similar programme targets mothers of children aged 6 to 13, who belong to the three lowest income quintiles. Both programmes have a relatively restricted coverage at present, limited to a small number of municipalities (Chile Atiende, n.d.[3]).

Families not covered by the above service options can opt for either (formal or informal) private daily care, or care provided by another family member. Informal care options are prevalent in rural areas, where many employed women – in agricultural co-operatives, for example – continue to entrust their children to relatives, even though they are eligible to receive a voucher for childcare. The same is true among single women who live within an extended family.

Support for the care of elderly and disabled individuals is predominantly restricted to the 60% most vulnerable households. The mission of the *Chile Cuida*, a sub-system of the Inter-Sectorial Social Protection System, is to accompany and support people in dependent situations, as well as their caregivers, and to promote networks through different services. Twenty municipalities participate in the system, which provides, among other services, technical assistance and training (Ministerio de Desarrollo Social y Família, n.d.[4]). A bill, currently under approval, foresees the creation of a disability insurance system relying on salary contributions of 0.2%.

Expanding opportunities of access to care could benefit both carers and the cared for. The long-term educational and social benefits of early childhood education and care may be particularly strong among children from disadvantaged families – often of cultural and linguistic minorities, for example – notably, by supporting preparations to formal schooling in primary school and preventing psychosocial problems (Nores and Barnett, 2010[5]; Heckman et al., 2010[6]). In Chile, girls and particularly boys who attended formal early childhood education and care programmes tend to perform strongly in standardised tests once they are in primary school (Cortázar, 2015[7]).Conversely, carers and institutions for disabled or elderly citizens or family members may be unprepared and overstretched, putting elderly and disabled people' mental and physical health at risk. In extreme cases, the resulting overload can contribute to cases of repeated violence against elderly people, including relatives. A 2012/2013 survey of the elderly in Veracruz and Santiago revealed that more than half of dependent seniors had experienced psychological violence and one in seven had suffered some form of neglect (SENAMA, 2013[8]).

Policy insights

Expand formal early childhood education and after-school care. The creation of a more universalised early childhood care system financed through a general employer contribution would be a step in the right direction. Under the current bill, employers of any size would contribute 0.1% of their employees' salaries to a central fund. Mothers and single fathers working more than 15 hours a week as employees or as self-employed workers affiliated with the social protection system would have access to the benefits. After applying, they could choose to send their children to a public or a private provider, the latter pending accreditation by the Ministry of Education. Costs of up to CLP 245 000 (around USD 315) per month would be covered by the fund. If the cost of the private day-care provider exceed this sum, parents would bear the remainder of the cost (Yévenes, 2018[9]).

Although the abolition of the size threshold would reduce the disincentives for hiring women, and could lead to a reduction of the wage penalty that women working for larger employers experience (IDB, 2015[10]), the current reform project has also attracted a number of criticisms. Some critics note that the new regime would not be universal, since it would exclude several groups, such as, for example, the students, along with part-time and public sector workers (although, in principle, the latter should have access to employer-provided childcare, this is not always the case). Partly related, other observers criticise the definition of childcare assistance used, according to which qualifying for the benefit depends upon the payment of a contribution, rather than being a basic right that is freely accessible by the most disadvantaged. Others note that, by making access contingent on labour status, the bill further entrenches the view that obligations for childcare is a prerogative of the workers, rather than being a social obligation. Finally, some lament that the voucher does not cover the full cost of private day care and that it undermines the public childcare sector.

A first step to addressing the above criticisms would be to grant the benefit to any child under the age of two, regardless of the labour status of the primary caregiver. As a further step, after the introduction of a right to care for under-two year olds, the right could also be extended to older children until they reach school age, although this would require a substantial expansion of the childcare infrastructure. Increasing the spots available in public day-care programmes can be one important way to expand coverage. Evidence from many OECD countries suggests that publicly funded childcare tends to have a more uniform quality and offer better working conditions to childcare workers (Moussié, 2016[11]). The process of opening new public day-care centres can be gradual, giving sufficient time to train and hire qualified personnel and to expand the public budget devoted to early childhood care and education. At the same time, private providers, which adhere to quality standards, can continue to play a role. Given that market rates for private day-care often exceed the planned maximum amount, lower- and middle-income families should have priority of access to public day care. In areas where these are over-subscribed and where a rapid expansion is impossible, the government could consider an additional subsidy for low- and middle-income families linked to the market rate of private providers.

Small companies that are currently below the 20 female employee threshold might oppose the introduction of an additional mandatory contribution, in particular at a time where they are struggling because of the COVID-19 pandemic and its economic fallout. One option to address this concern could be to phase in the introduction, with longer lead-up times for companies that can demonstrate that the COVID-19 crisis strongly affected their revenues. In addition, an information campaign demonstrating the benefits to the firms themselves could support the introduction of the new regime. For example, case studies from textile companies in Jordan and Viet Nam showed that staff turnover and sick leave declined by a third and 9%, respectively, when the companies started offering workplace childcare. A recent report by the International Finance Corporation, provides further examples on the business case for employer-supported childcare, by showing the benefits that employers gained from providing the service (International Finance Corporation, 2017[12]).

In addition to expanded care options for pre-school children, families also need more options for qualified after-school care. To this effect, a further expansion of the 4-7 programme to all municipalities and income quintiles would represent a desirable option. This would expand the opportunities for parents to work full-time.

Investing in long-term care. Lessening the burden of care for elderly and disabled family members can go a long way towards supporting women's access to labour markets. Ideally, this would require expanding the *Chile Cuida* programme, both geographically and across income groups. As one tool in this direction, easing access to information on services available locally can be a way to point families towards resources that could help them. For example, in La Plata in Argentina, a network of residents, academic experts and service providers created a website to provide such information. Respite care and training, aimed at providing short-term relief to families of any income category, is another tool. In Belo Horizonte in Brazil, for example, social and health workers spend a week in a family to allow carers to recover and to learn how to best care for their relatives (UN Women, 2017[13]). In addition to such temporary relief efforts, it is important to invest in long-term care infrastructure and insurance. With an ageing population, the need for more support in the form of regular visits by trained care workers, or of institutional care, is likely to increase. In this context, public oversight is a key to ensure the enforcement of care standards, as well as labour standards, for paid care workers, many of whom are women. A long-term care insurance programme, financed either through taxes or through a social insurance, could help pay for care. To keep costs in check, the eligibility and benefit limits can initially be quite restrictive, paying only in cases where the family is not able to finance the care for severely ill or disabled family members (Rhee, Done and Anderson, 2015[14]).

Expanding parental leave and flexible work options

Parental leave policies affect family decisions about the division of paid and unpaid work between partners. When there is no maternity leave, mothers may have to drop out of the labour force and subsequently find it difficult to re-enter. In OECD countries, the female employment rate rises slightly with the length of the statutory maternity leave but starts to fall when the duration exceeds two years. This underscores that beyond a certain limit, excessively long maternity leave periods may be counter-productive, leading to a widening of the gender employment gap, rather than shrinking it (Thévenon and Solaz, 2013[15]). It also brings to attention the important balancing role that fathers can play by taking paternity leave and their contribution to counter the frequent pattern whereby couples revert to a traditional division of labour when they become parents. For example, in Norway, couples whose child was born four weeks after the introduction of paternity leave reported fewer conflicts about the division of unpaid work and some improvements in the sharing of housework tasks than couples whose child was born just beforehand (Kotsadam and Finseraas, 2011[16]). Evidence from Sweden and Spain likewise suggests that couples split unpaid work more equally following the introduction of more gender-equal parental leave policies (Hagqvist et al., 2017[17]). A detailed analysis from Germany shows that fathers who took parental leave decreased their paid work afterwards and increased the hours devoted to childcare. However, only fathers who took more than two months of leave also increased the involvement in other types of unpaid work (Bünning, 2015[18]).

The leave available to parents in Chile exceeds the regional average. It involves a paid maternity leave of 18 weeks, which exceeds the minimum defined by the 2000 ILO Convention No. 183 on Maternity Protection and fulfils the recommendation of ILO Recommendation No. 191 (Figure 2.2). In addition, as one of the few countries in Latin America, Chile offers 12 weeks of parental leave. Half of this parental leave is reserved for mothers, while the other half can be taken by fathers as well. Part-time parental leave of 18 weeks at 50% of net pay is also an option.

In other ways, however, the leave system is not as flexible as elsewhere and lacks coverage. Six weeks of maternity leave have to be taken prenatally and mothers and fathers cannot take parental leave concurrently. Since the costs of maternity leave are borne by the social security system, informal workers, not affiliated with the system, cannot benefit. Detailed analysis of the coverage capacity of the system suggests that in 2015 only 44% of mothers received maternity benefits (IPC-IG and UNICEF., 2020[19]). During the COVID-19 crisis, the government and the opposition co-operated to pass a law to extend paid parental leave to 90 days. To be eligible, the regular parental leave had to end after 18 March. Moreover, primary caretakers of children born after 2013 can ask for a leave of absence during which they are entitled to receive emergency family assistance (24 Horas, 2020[20]).

Dedicated paternity leave at childbirth in Chile only amounts to five working days, though it can be extended using part of the parental leave. The five days are slightly above the regional average, but far below the OECD average (Figure 2.2). However, it is important to note that the OECD average of around eight weeks reflects in part the extremely high entitlements of one year of paternity leave in Korea and Japan. Very few men in either of the two countries take any paternity leave, let alone during a one year period (Rich, 2019[21]). In Chile, the Commission on Women and Gender Equity launched an initiative to increase paternity leave to 30 days, 15 of which would be taken straight after the birth and 15 at any time in the first six months (Cámara de Diputadas y Diputados, 2019[22]).

Figure 2.2. The duration of parental leave in Chile is generous compared to the region but not the OECD average

Maternity leave in weeks and paternity leave in days, 2018 or latest available

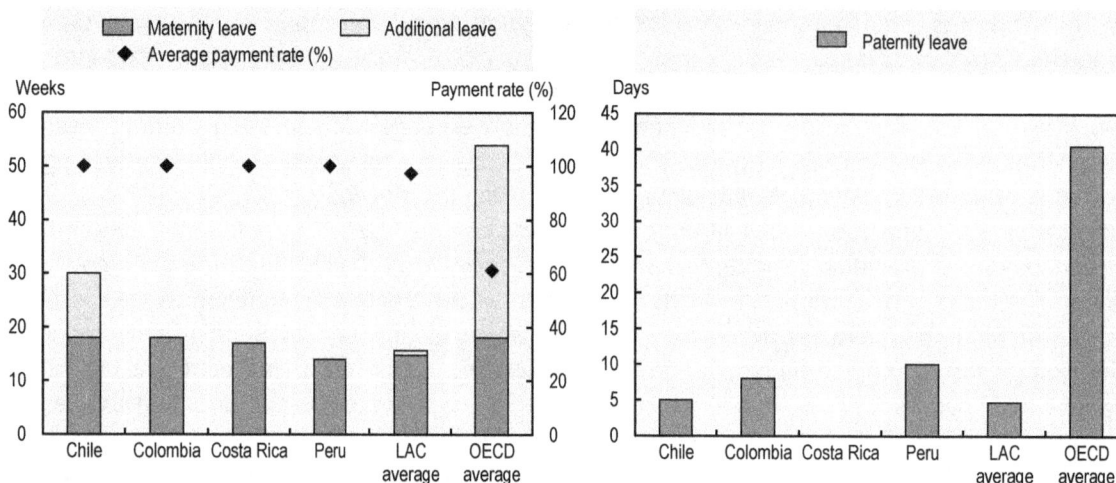

Note: The Latin American and Caribbean (LAC) and OECD averages are unweighted. The 12 weeks of additional leave in Chile can be taken by either mothers or fathers and can be extended to 18 weeks at 50% rather than 100% of pay. Values for Latin American countries generally refer to the leave that workers in the formal sector are eligible for. The weeks of paternity leave are multiplied by five to arrive at a daily value, assuming a five-day working week. The OECD average is based on the sum of paternity leave and parental leave reserved for fathers.
Source: OECD (n.d.[23]), "Table PF2.1.A. Summary of paid leave entitlements available to mothers" and "Table PF2.1.B. Summary of paid leave entitlements for fathers", *OECD Family Database*, http://www.oecd.org/els/soc/PF2_1_Parental_leave_systems.xlsx and IPC-IG and UNICEF (2020[19]), "Table 6: Duración y beneficios de las licencias (regímenes generales)", *Maternidad y Paternidad en el lugar de trabajo en América Latina y el Caribe – Políticas para la licencia de maternidad y paternidad y apoyo a la lactancia maternal".*

Once back to work, parents have limited options to ease the time-crunch of simultaneously working and taking care of children. At 45 hours for full-time and 30 hours for part-time work, maximum work hours are above the standard work week of 40 hours common to many OECD countries. In addition, many workers work longer hours. In Latin America in the mid-2010s, 21.4% worked more than 48 hours and 8.1% worked more than 60 hours (ILO, 2018[24]). In Chile in 2013, 17% and 8% of male and female employees, respectively, worked more than 48 hours per week (Yañez, 2016[25]). The respective share increased to 29% and 19% among own-account workers. These figures do not take into account the time for commuting and the – at least – ten hours that a full-time worker normally devotes to childcare. Unsurprisingly, in this context, many families opt for the traditional one-breadwinner model: as depicted by Table 1.1, Chapter 1, in nearly half of two parent households with at least one child under the age of 14, one person does not work at all and this is typically the woman.

Few Chileans benefit from flexible work options. The recently introduced Act on Distance Work and Teleworking (March 2020) represents a step in the right direction, since it stipulates that the workers who opt for this arrangement benefit from all rights established in the Labour Code, while the right to disconnect is also recognised (ILO, 2020[26]). A pilot project launched by the National Institute for Industrial Property in 2017 investigated the possibilities of teleworking in the public sector (Soto et al., 2018[27]). In addition to recognising the importance of the quality of the physical and technological infrastructure as a pre-condition of success, the pilot project identified the crucial roles played by effective strategies of communication and training to engage civil servants. In Europe, around a third of employees can decide when they start and stop teleworking with a margin of autonomy, and more than 60% can take one or two hours off for personal or family reasons (OECD, 2016[28]). However, teleworking was not particularly common in Europe prior to the COVID-19 crisis: only one in five employees in 2015 had worked from home at least once over the 12 months prior to the outbreak.

Policy insights

Establish reserved paternity leave weeks as part of parental leave. Although Chile already has parental leave that either men or women can benefit from, as elsewhere, few fathers actually take the leave. Several European countries (including Iceland and Sweden) have successfully boosted their take-up through reserving a certain share of the parental leave for fathers, meaning that the total leave that a couple can use is longer if both take it. Another policy option is to lengthen paternity leave, which can per definition not be transferred to the mother (OECD, 2019[29])

Support the policies to increase the coverage of maternity and paternity benefits by stepping up the momentum of the broader policies to strengthen formalisation. This is important to ensure that parental leave be accessible to all workers, including the less protected ones. Currently, many new parents in Chile are not entitled to paid parental leave because they work without a formal contract and lack social insurance coverage. This situation underscores that the enforcement of parental leave arrangements would hardly generate sizeable results in terms of coverage if conducted in isolation from the broader policies to strengthen formalisation in Chile.

- As a key priority, it would be important to keep the momentum of ongoing policy efforts to boost formal employment. Although an analysis of the policies to achieve this long-term objective is beyond the remit of this work, the broad requirements include making social security contributions progressive, increasing labour inspections and accurate monitoring of results (OECD, 2018[30]).

- As part of these contextual policies, the government could consider prioritising sectors known for the relatively widespread presence of informality and the over-representation of female employment. These include a range of service activities, from personal care and household services, for example, to restaurants and hotels. As one regional example in the particular area of household services, Argentina has introduced a comprehensive set of measures to extend the coverage of social protection to domestic workers. These involve the introduction of mandatory written contracts, the dissemination of booklets that describe domestic workers' rights, and the possibility for the employers to deduct the social security contributions paid on behalf of the domestic workers. These initiatives combine with awareness raising campaigns, with letters being written to high-income households reminding them of their obligation to declare any workers (Lexartza, Chaves and Cardeco, 2016[31]). If Chile were to follow a similar approach, it could consider providing tax-funded benefits to allow informally employed women eligible for the *Chile Crece Contigo* programme – which includes the promotion of active parenthood among its missions – receiving some limited paid benefits to take time off their jobs. Another potentially attractive option, particularly to the self-employed, could consist in the introduction of a contribution subsidy again intended to allow taking time off jobs.

Strengthen flexible work options. Depending on the type of job, flexible starting times and teleworking can reduce the time crunch that parents experience due to long working hours, commutes and family obligations. Compared to many other countries in the region, Chile has better prerequisites for teleworking in terms of its internet infrastructure and its recent teleworking laws have positive features. The government can encourage this process even further through multiple measures. For example, it can financially support those firms willing to invest in their ICT infrastructure; provide digital skills training in rural areas; and implement information campaigns that show the benefits of teleworking while also equipping managers with the skills on how to communicate effectively with employees that they see less frequently. (OECD, 2020[32]).

Reducing the transmission of gender stereotypes through the education system

There is a vast literature on attitudes about gender roles, how they are transmitted to children, including the role that stereotypes play in influencing the educational and occupational choices of girls and boys (OECD, 2012[33]; Karlson and Simonsson, 2011[34]; Wahlstrom, 2003[35]). As noted above, girls may shy away from choosing educational tracks and occupations perceived as traditionally masculine, such as STEM degree programmes (OECD, 2015[36]). Given that occupations characterised by a strong presence of male workers are often better paid, these choices can permanently hamper women's earning potential (Kunze, 2018[37]). At the same time, boys brought up to believe in traditional gender roles may gravitate away from care professions (OECD, 2017[38]), and may be less willing to participate in housework and child care activities once they are adults (Lachance-Grzela and Bouchard, 2010[39]).

A stereotype-free educational approach can allow boys and girls acquiring full awareness of their strengths, along with the tools to nurture them so as to be able to pursue their interests and aspirations freely throughout the life cycle (UNESCO, 2004[40]). This positive approach rests on two notions:

- The first is that the education system has a key role to play in tackling the persistence of gender stereotypes (Bousseau and Tap, 1998[41]; OECD, 2012[33]). For example, even though girls have gained access to schooling on a similar scale to boys in many countries, curricula and school materials have not followed through, implying that the representation of gender roles continues to be the same, using the old archetypes. Research has shown that in textbooks, men often appear in a wide variety of professional (paid) roles and women in domestic (unpaid) roles (EU, 2012[42]). A stereotype-free educational approach can significantly help addressing these gaps and their transmission between generations.

- The second concept assumes that the potential for teachers to support students' self-image, confidence and life paths remains largely underused, at present. A number of studies reveal that the attitude of the teachers affects the interest of the students in school subjects, influencing, in turn, career orientations (OECD, 2012[33]; OECD, 2015[36]). If teachers do not trust girls' scientific abilities and provide them with less encouraging feedbacks, for example, girls' success and interest in these subjects can be reduced (OXFAM, 2005[43]) (OXFAM, 2007[44]). For Chile, a study by the Ministry of Women and the National Women's Service (SERNAM) (2009[45]) showed that teachers often address classes using masculine forms (such as "boys" and the male forms for all children and students, regardless of the gender). When giving examples, they tend to confine female characters to the "private world" spheres, namely the domestic, maternal and care settings, with male characters placed in the "public world" settings where fully-fledged economic activities take place.

Addressing discriminatory practices in the educational sector is a key component of the broader policies for promoting equal opportunities for men and women that the Chilean Government is pursuing. The efforts to revise the national curriculum date back to the turn of the century. They involved initiative aimed at levelling the visibility of both genders in textbooks, at promoting more participatory work methodologies in the classrooms, and widening the recourse to mixed work groups. More recently, the 2014-18 government programme recommended a gender-aware approach throughout all educational levels. In addition, the initiative *Eduquemos con Igualdad* (Let's educate with equality), launched in 2016 by the Ministry of Education and Comunidad Mujer – a civil society organisation that promotes the rights of women – included guidelines for tackling educators' gender biases and behaviours and for strengthening the engagement of parents in the creation of a gender-sensitive education (MINEDUC, 2018[46]). As another milestone, the 2015-18 plan on "Education for Gender Equality" identified patterns that reproduce gender stereotypes and inequalities (UDP, 2018[47]) and presented proposals for adapting the ongoing National Educational Reform to reflect the gender perspective (MINEDUC, 2015[48]). The resulting 2019 pre-school curriculum increased the representation of female writers or authors (Ministerio del Interior y de la Seguridad Publica, 2018[49]). With support of the National Women's Service (SERNAM), the Ministry of Education (MINEDUC) developed a manual of guidelines to prevent gender biases in textbooks for distribution among publishers. The creation of training sessions facilitated the dissemination of the guidelines.

Recent assessments of the progress achieved provided an opportunity to take stock of the progress achieved. It revealed a number of areas where difficulties persist, particularly there remains scope for more concrete actions to integrate the gender perspective into the secondary curriculum (UDP, 2018[47]). In 2018, the Ministry of Education created a commission of experts with the task to identify gender biases in the curricula across levels of education, from preschool to high school. Although the findings have not been published, the commission has made several immediate and long-term recommendations to the government (MINEDUC, 2019[50]). These recommendations include expanding the gender-sensitive perspective to secondary education.

Policy insights

Introduce trainings to help teachers becoming more mindful about the importance of gender attitudes and stereotypes at school. One lesson from the international experience is that the efforts to create a culture conducive to gender equality should start from early education and with the willing support of the teachers (OECD, 2012[33]). Specific training is important to help the teachers adapting their pedagogical approaches to the age group of the children (UNESCO, 2017[51]). For example, teachers have played a pivotal role in the initiatives undertaken by the government of the Flanders (Belgium) to raise awareness about gender roles in Flemish schools. Teachers received trainings to detect the presence of gender attitudes and stereotypes in the curriculum material and were encouraged to propose solutions on how to improve the situation. There is evidence of teachers having subsequently become more mindful of the importance to avert the use of a spoken language with the children that could favour the development of stereotyped gender roles. Assignments that could reinforce the development of identity aspects (girls to carry out organisational and support roles such as taking notes, planning events, co-ordinating group work, and so on) have gradually diminished. These outcomes were helped by changing the organisation of the classrooms and making recourse to mixed groups to limit splitting boys and girls (Council of Europe, 2014[52]). The lessons from this experience provide a potentially useful benchmark against which to assess the pedagogical guides issued by the Chilean Government and progress with implementation.

Engage the families in the process of creating gender-sensitive education. Although the main responsibility rely on schools when educating future citizens, involving parents is key when introducing a new educational approach aimed at strengthening gender-sensitive education. The family often acts as "spokesperson" of entrenched prejudices and parents could view the new initiatives to change course with suspicion. One positive feature of the pedagogical guidance implemented by the Chilean Government lies in the fact that it invites teachers to take a more pro-active role by exploring options for co-operative forms of engagement with Parents' Associations. Upfront engagement to raise the consciousness of parents could spill over to households, smoothing the transmission of traditional gender roles within the larger family. The Chilean pedagogical guides include a video for parents to watch ahead of discussion meetings as a tool to prepare their thoughts.

As one example of international practices to engage parents, in Peru the Ministry of Education launched a national campaign in 2019 to inform parents about the importance of mainstreaming gender-sensitive practices in education and their interactions with the curriculum. Almost 140 information centres opened to explain families how and why the gender approach is implemented in the education curriculum (MINEDUC, 2019[53]). In Ireland, as part of the gender mainstreaming strategy, the Ministry of Education and Science developed guidelines, which address the whole school community, including parents. The guidelines for primary and secondary schools provide parents with information about school obligations in relation to equality legislation, explanation of gender mainstreaming and what it entails and suggestions for actions that parents can undertake at schools (Council of Europe, 2011[54]; EIGE, 2020[55]).

Keeping the momentum for change is essential, given that fighting gender stereotypes through the education system is a long-term process. Enhancing gender equality in education is a long-term process that requires capitalising on present and previous efforts to promote improvements. By implication, continuous monitoring of achievements can be of great value to put Chile on a sustainable path of progress. As part of a defined long-term strategy, Chile could identify a clear set of intermediate targets and standards, against which to organise an independent monitoring body in charge of assessing progress and disseminating success stories at school.

Box 2.1. Summary of policy options for reducing barriers to sharing paid and unpaid work equitably in Chile

A range of institutional, legal and cultural constraints lies in the way of reducing the barriers to achieving a more equitable sharing of unpaid work activities in Chile. The OECD suggests:

Create a more comprehensive care system

- *Expand formal early childhood education and after-school care.* The current bill aims at the creation of a more universalised early childhood care system by abolishing the size threshold according to which employers with more than 20 female workers must provide childcare assistance to children under the age of two.

- *Invest in long-term care.* As an immediate objective, this could require expanding the *Chile Cuida* programme, both geographically and across income groups. Easing access to information on services available in the local area can be a way to point families towards resources that could help them.

Expand parental leave and flexible work options

- *Establish reserved paternity leave weeks as part of the parental leave.* Although Chile already has parental leave that either men or women can use, few fathers actually take the leave. Many European countries have had success with boosting their take-up through reserving a certain share of the parental leave for fathers, meaning that the total leave that a couple can use is longer if both take it.

- Support the policies to increase the coverage of maternity and paternity benefits by stepping up the momentum of the broader policies to strengthen formalisation. Currently, many new parents in Chile are not entitled to paid parental leave because they work without a formal contract and lack social insurance coverage. This situation underscores that the enforcement of parental leave arrangements would hardly generate sizeable results in terms of coverage if conducted in isolation from the broader policies to strengthen formalisation in Chile.

- *Strengthen flexible work options.* Depending on the type of job, flexible starting times and teleworking can reduce the time crunch experienced by parents, reflecting long working hours, commutes and family obligations. The recent teleworking laws has positive features that the government could strengthen even further, for example, by financially supporting firms willing to invest in their ICT infrastructure and digital skills training in rural areas

Reduce the transmission of gender stereotypes through the education system

- *Introduce training to help teachers becoming more mindful about gender attitudes and stereotypes at school.* One lesson from the international experience is that the efforts to create a culture conducive to gender equality should start from early education and with the willing support of the teachers. Specific training is important to help teachers adapting their pedagogical approaches to the age group of the children.

- ● ***Engage the families in the process of creating gender-sensitive education.*** One positive feature of the pedagogical guidance implemented by the Chilean Government lies in the fact that it invites teachers to take a more pro-active role by exploring options for co-operative forms of engagement with the Parents' Associations. Upfront engagement to raise the consciousness of parents could spill over to the households, smoothing the transmission of traditional gender roles within the larger family.

- ● ***Keep the momentum for change by identifying clear intermediate targets and standards.*** An independent monitoring body could be in charge of assessing progress and disseminating success stories among schools.

Making women's paid work pay more

Ensuring access to quality education for all

As discussed in the review of the evidence section, different factors explain the particularly high risk being faced by young women in Chile to be NEETs, nearly twice more pronounced than observed among young men (see Figure 1.12, Chapter 1). For example, women often have no other choice but to drop out of school in case of teenage pregnancy or to renounce participating in the labour market altogether following childbirth in young adulthood.

The Chilean Ministry of Education has a number of policies to address drop-outs from school, including due to premature motherhood. The public and private schools that do not comply with the statutory recognised right of pregnant students and mothers to remain in school (recognised since 2009) are subject to a fine (MINEDUC, 2018[56]). The Ministry of Education's protocol for the retention of students in the school system exempts pregnant students, as well as teenage mothers and fathers, from the standard requirement of 85% minimum attendance. It also sets out guidelines for facilitating the establishment of support networks involving parents and guardians. Furthermore, it mandates the school to respect the breastfeeding schedule of mothers (MINEDUC, 2019[57]). The Ministry of Education monitors the outcomes of these policies using a School Retention indicator (MINEDUC, 2016[58]), which allows tracking the capacity of the schools to identify and support students at risk of dropping out early. Evidence of an increase in the number of student drop-outs during the COVID-19 pandemic, has accelerated the introduction of a new pilot scheme to provide special support for students at a particular risk of dropping out of the school system, using scholarships, ensuring pedagogical and psychological support, and communicating the benefits of completing studies. As part of this, in nine regions of the country interdisciplinary teams of social and psychological pedagogues work with youth particularly exposed to socio-educational risks. A joint programme between the Ministry of Social Development and the Ministry of Education through the government agency Junaeb (Junta Nacional de Auxilio Escolar y Becas – National Board of School Aid and Scholarships) has similar objectives.

Preventive educational programmes have a key role to play in lowering the exposure of teenage girls to the risk of becoming pregnant. One welcome feature of the programmes implemented by Chile lies in the fact that they reach out to both boys and girls. In addition, the delivery of the services extends beyond the premises of the schools as a way of broadening coverage. One example is the programme Espacios Amigables, which the Ministry of Health co-ordinates with the support of the network of local Family Health Centers (CESFAM). The programme involves the provision of various assistance services to adolescents from 10 to 19 years old, ranging from health care, safe nutrition and sexual education, particularly targeting youth who are less likely to use other health facilities due to various barriers (scheduling, long waiting times, confidentiality, and so on). In a friendly care space, set with youthful taste, adolescents can meet trained staff in privacy. A friendly approach in an adapted space is important to make girls and boys feel that they can safely and comfortably raise questions, clarify doubts and address concerns. Additionally, workshops on sexual reproductive health and mental health are held in schools and community spaces, at convenient times that do not overlap with school hours. Moreover, the *Programa Salud Integral Adolescentes y Jóvenes* is a comprehensive programme that aims at improving access to, and offer of health care services by, adolescents and young people up to the age of 24 years. It has a gender sensitive focus, in the field of prevention, treatment and rehabilitation, involving families and the community.

Policy insights

Provide additional support to vulnerable girls and teenage mothers. Chile has made progress towards ensuring that teenage mothers stay in education and raising the impact of the policies to reduce underage/young pregnancies. Initiatives, such as the programme *Espacios Amigables* and the *Plan de Salud Integral de Adolescencia*, have helped in this direction by integrating prevention and education policies more closely. This is essential to combat teen pregnancies and to limit, in turn, school drop-outs.

In perspective, there could be scope for providing additional financial support to mothers and their young children as a way of ensuring that they acquire basic education and skills that they can use at work. For example, a programme in Uruguay aims at promoting educational projects for mothers under the age of 23 by providing financial support for the care of their children while on education and training. In Australia, the government offers a variety of transfer programmes to teenage parents, such as the JET Child Care Fee Assistance subsidy, for example, which allows mothers to pay for formal childcare during the completion of their studying curriculum and the transition to work. The amount, paid directly to childcare providers, is commensurate to the income of the household, the child's age and the hours of recognised activities by the mother and her partner.

The findings of recent analysis for Colombia by Cortés, Gallego and Maldonado (2016) provide some useful guidance for programme design in that they suggest that, in order for Conditional Cash Transfer programmes to support the reduction of fertility rates among adolescents, they should be "conditional enough". This requires the use of well-stated and enforceable pre-defined criteria to track school success and attendance. In Chile, the protocol for the retention of students in the school system rightly exempts pregnant students, as well as teenage mothers and fathers, from the standard requirement of 85% minimum attendance. Nevertheless, the findings of this study suggest that the observance of some form of conditionality might be advisable to qualify for the transfers. For example, the government could require that students complete the school year and enrol in the following grade in order to continue benefitting from the assistance and/or that the subsidy cannot be recuperated after too long an interruption of the programme.

Ensure comprehensive sexual education and information at school. Even though the right to sexual information and education in secondary schools in Chile has been guaranteed by law since 2010 (Ley 20.480), actual implementation is left to the discretion of each institutions, which can vary depending upon local convictions and beliefs. In addition, there is no minimum curriculum requirement and when taught, sexual education often focusses on biological differences, without preventive reproductive information. Since many parents do not communicate with their children about this topic, most teenagers inform themselves from the internet, often leading to misinformation and distorted views, which could affect emotional development (Obrach King, Alexandra et al., 2017[59]). A better way to support the sexual information of students is by guaranteeing a minimum curriculum on sexual and preventive education in every school and monitoring its implementation (UNESCO, 2018[60]). Moreover, a special advisor on health and sexual education inside schools could equip students with appropriate information. It is preferable that the advisor be a trained young person, with whom the students can more easily identify as a peer, rather than a regular teacher with whom they are likely to feel uncomfortable.

Reward and communicate the benefits of completing studies. Free education is a necessary pre-condition to decrease the cost of sending children to school, especially for poor families. However, free access to education may not be sufficient since the subjective perception of the benefits of school enrolment varies across households. To account for this, conditional cash transfers (CCTs) could provide regular transfer benefits to parents of poor backgrounds who choose to keep their children at school. Meta-analysis of 94 studies from 47 CCTs programmes shows that school drop-outs tend to diminish when the benefits are contingent upon school enrolments and attendances. Qualifying for the benefits is typically associated with an 80-90% attendance obligation. The benefits also reduce the exposure of children to child labour.

Many girls and women lack the motivation to complete their education curriculum because they lack the support to develop a clear professional project. This consideration applies even more strongly to girls who are in secondary education but are already aware that their performance levels in the national test score will unlikely be high enough to qualify them to enroll in public tertiary education. School mentoring, student counselling and targeted scholarships are a key to helping girls and young women to remain and continue in education. One example of good practice is the Girls' Network Mentoring Programme introduced by the United Kingdom. The aim of this initiative is to connect young girls between 14 and 19 years old and from disadvantaged schools with women from a range of established business activities. This mentoring allows girls to acquire information and building networks that would otherwise be impossible for them to access by relying solely on their own school and circle of family and friends. More than 500 mentors give practical advice and help girls with guidance about careers and university applications. Mentors receive a special training programme and, once girls complete their year-long mentoring journey, they graduate to become lifelong ambassadors of the programme.

Promoting women in non-traditional careers and leadership positions

The extent to which the election of a female President over two Presidential terms – President Michelle Bachelet, 2006-10 and subsequently 2014-18 – has contributed to changing the template of male-dominated politics in Chile is difficult to assess precisely. However, it is certain that a female leadership has represented a symbol of cultural change, which has fuelled a new momentum for greater equality and participation in all areas of public life (Albornoz Pollmann, 2017[61]). A quota law entered into force in 2017, as part of a broader electoral reform, with political parties being required to field no fewer than 40% of female candidates.

Importantly, the results of the Constitutional referendum in October 2020 set Chile to become the first country in the world to have as many female as male participants in its Constitutional Convention (Senado, 2019[62]; GOB, 2020[63]). International experience shows that although the participation of women in similar constitutional reforms has increased overtime, it still falls far short from parity with men. For example, in the 75 countries that engaged in constitutional reforms between 1990 and 2015 (including transitions from authoritarianism to democracy), only 19% of the members of the constitutional bodies were women (IPI, 2015[64]). The level of participation and inclusion in a constitution-making process can affect legitimacy, as well as, prospectively, the degree to which women will be able to represent their specific interests in the future (Philipps, 1998[65]; IDEA, 2019[66]; Hart, 2003[67]).

The above patterns have spilled over to the policies that influence the access of women to leadership and management positions in the business sector and could potentially set the tone for more future improvements. Following the introduction of a 40% target of women on the boards of state-owned enterprises – first set during President Bachelet's two Presidencies and further enforced during the two Presidencies of President Pinera –, the actual percentage reached 42.1% in 2018 (Comunidad Mujer, 2018[68]). However, even though this achievement should have encouraged the private companies to emulate the experience of the state-owned enterprises, there is evidence that the record of accomplishments is still modest across the private sector. For the 40 largest companies rated in the stock market, the share of women on boards was a meagre 6.2% in 2018 (Comunidad Mujer, 2018[68]). A recent requirement by the Superintendencia de Valores y Seguros (SVS, Superintendence of Securities and Insurance) seeks to generate more information on the progress made by the private sector towards the standards of the public sector. In particular, "rule 385" provides on the adoption of social responsibility and sustainable development policies, referring in particular to the diversity in the composition of the board of directors and in the appointment of the company's main executives (Sistema de Empresas, 2016[69]).

There are indications suggesting that the policy dialogue can foster the participation of women at all levels of governance in the private sector. A glance at the transport and mining sectors, which in addition to being economically important in Chile have a strong male-dominated tradition, seems to corroborate this view. The pay-off of gender-equity policies have been relatively significant in transport, likelihood reflecting the fact that the Ministry of Transport and Telecommunications and the sector associations decided to implement an ambitious gender equality strategy following a concerted implementation approach. In stark contrast, the participation of women in the governance remains relatively low in mining companies, which possibly reflects a less dialogue-centred approach, notwithstanding the abolition of the law that forbade women from working in the sector dates back to 1996.

In Chile, many women who opt for scientific careers struggle to combine the fulfilment of a lengthy and demanding academic curriculum with family responsibilities. Doctoral students and post-docs, for example, generally lack the rights to maternity benefits and pre- and post-natal care. In addition, the concentration of research activities in a few urban centres and the 'excellence' criteria for scholarships imply that it is difficult for more disadvantaged students to gain access to prestigious university programmes. Although these difficulties are common to both genders, for girls they appear compounded by higher care obligations and the impact of stereotypes.

The Chilean Government, the universities and research institutions have introduced a series of initiatives to increase the attractiveness of STEM careers to women. The year 2019 saw the launch of the campaign *Mas Mujeres en Ciencias* (More Women in Sciences) jointly organised by the Ministry of Women and Gender Equity and the Ministry of Sciences, Technology, Knowledge and Innovation. This initiative seeks to encourage female presence in historically masculinised professional careers. The Institutional Policy on Gender, issued by the National Commission on Scientific and Technological Research's (CONICYT) and covering the eight year period between 2017 and 2025, aims to expand maternity leave rights for junior researchers and to improve the representation of female scientists in decision-making positions, for instance as heads of research groups (CONICYT, 2017[70]). Since 2020, the Ministry of Science includes a special Council for Gender Equity, delegated to elaborate action plans for gender equality in STEM. In 2013, the Faculty of Mathematical and Physical Sciences at the University of Chile created a gender equality admissions programme, which has led to increase the share of admitted women into its competitive engineering and science programme from 19% to 32%.

Policy insights

Strengthen women's representation at the executive level in private sector companies. The system of a gender quota and targets has shown positive results in Chile's congress and state-owned enterprises. However, the enforcement of similar quotas or voluntary targets on boards and in senior management positions remains difficult among private sector companies (OECD, 2019[71]). International practice shows that one way of supporting and accelerating the inclusion of women in leadership positions and eliminating wage gaps is by requiring companies to disclose statistics on the gender composition at different management levels. Further to encouraging the dissemination of good practices, disclosure can result in "name and shame" effects, by allowing singling out non-compliant companies. In Germany, the 2015 Act on equal participation of women and men in executive positions in private and public sectors set a 30% gender diversity quota for supervisory boards and required listed and co-determined companies (where workers can vote for representatives on the board) to establish targets for gender equality at the top two levels of management. Israeli state-owned enterprises have a legal target of appropriate representation for both genders on the board of directors – usually 50%, unless there is a sound reason why such representation is unachievable. Until reaching the goal, priority is for directors of the under-represented gender with a possibility to fine non-complying companies.

Step up monitoring and evaluation mechanisms. Specific and measurable objectives are a key to evaluate whether goals for women's representation in different professions and at the leadership level are met. For example, strong internal monitoring mechanisms could support the goal of an equal pay for an equivalent work. In Australia, the Workplace Gender Equality Act requires non-public sector employers with 100 or more employees to disclose their "Gender Equality Indicators" in annual filings submitted to the Workplace Gender Equality Agency.

Raise girls' interest in science, technology and mathematics. Students should become aware of STEM before moving to post-secondary education to be able to make informed decisions about future careers. Mentorship programmes can allow them to identify positive role models, including by drawing inspiration from high-level positions in public and private companies. By shaping girls' career goals and enhancing perceptions that those goals are on reach, the impact of positive examples can be significant. In addition, mentorship programmes increase self-confidence, boost communication skills, and enhance leadership qualities more durably, which will benefit girls during their careers. In 2017 the OECD and the Mexican Government created the "NinaSTEMPueden" initiative for the promotion of conferences, workshops and mentorship programmes to enhance the attractiveness of STEM curricula to Mexican girls (OECD, 2020[72]).

Aside from mentorship, school textbooks could disseminate examples of male and female scientists, while introducing experimental and interactive science experiences at school could also help to increase girls' interest in STEM. The University of Costa Rica, for example, has organised several science workshops for 7-13 year-old girls in 2019. Public awareness campaigns can support the general fight against traditional gender stereotypes by showing that excelling in STEM areas is compatible with family life. These campaigns should start at the earliest stage of education, including with the support of social media platforms. TV programmes and series promoting women role models in STEM could be a source of inspiration for young girls.

Recognise and reinforce the application of statutory maternity and paternity leave in the academic sector and support access to care services. Expanding these rights, as proposed by the roadmap for fostering the representation of women in science as set out by the Ministry of Science, can foster the attractiveness of academic careers to female science graduates. Mothers who return to work after their maternity leave should have the option to increase their working hours gradually.

Supporting female entrepreneurship

As discussed in the review of the evidence section, women in Chile are less likely to be entrepreneurs than men. While the proportion of men and women who are own-account workers is virtually the same, the share of those who are employers is about twice as large among men than women. Moreover, women entrepreneurs are much less likely to own or manage medium and large firms. Furthermore, recent analyses of the traits for starting a business suggest that women more likely than men become entrepreneur because they cannot find good employment alternatives. By contrast, men are more likely do so because they have identified a good business opportunity.

Women face higher barriers to entrepreneurship than men do in Chile. As discussed above, one important barrier stems as a side effect of a very restrictive marital law, which implies that is difficult for married women to start or close a business without the consent of their husbands (OECD, 2020[73]). Without consent, the woman cannot access the collateral, which undermines creditworthiness. Accordingly, a woman entrepreneur faces a higher risk of being subject to an interest rate penalty when launching a new business.

It is unfortunate that marital law stands in the way of women gaining access to financing, because it means that women have more difficulty to access existing support programmes (OEAP, 2018[74]) as per the short review below:

- Launched in November 2019, the *Fondo Lévantate Mujer* of the Women's Promotion and Development Foundation (PRODEMU) supports the entrepreneurship of more than 600 women through providing 250 000 Chilean pesos (approximately EUR 290) as a "seed financing" to enable the launch of new businesses.

- The programme *Mujer Emprende* of the Ministry of Women, launched in 2015, targets female entrepreneurs whose businesses have existed for at least one year. Through the *Escuela Mujer Emprende*, the programme seeks to strengthen the business skills of these entrepreneurs. There are three different levels of training, depending on how developed the business is. It also seeks to strengthen the networks of female entrepreneurs. Around 1 000 women have participated in the programme to date.

- The programme *Yo Emprendo Semilla* (previously *Programa de Apoyo al Microemprendimiento*), run by the Ministry of Social Development, is open to individuals from vulnerable households who have a potentially promising business idea. The programme provides around USD 600 in start-up capital, 60 hours of training and follow-up mentoring visits. An evaluation of the programme found that participation boosted employment, business practices and labour income in the short- and long-term. Compared to the control group, including individuals who did not receive the subsidy, the probability of still being self-employed 45 months later was higher among those who received a larger subsidy, although individuals who qualified for a smaller subsidy were more likely to be in wage employment (Martínez A., Puentes and Ruiz-Tagle, 2018[75]).

- The Ministry of the Economy offers a technical co-operation service for small (SERCOTEC) and larger companies (CORFO). For example, it provides training, subsidies, and advice on accessing foreign markets. The SERCOTEC and CORFO programmes are open to men and women alike, but the subsidies of CORFO are 10% higher for women.

In addition to the impact of the marital law, the barriers to entrepreneurship include fewer opportunities for training and for accessing financial resources. Business networks are typically smaller and less effective for many women, particularly from low-income households. The lack of training opportunities, the difficulties to participate in networking events and to access financing sources, compound the impact of overburdening domestic responsibilities, travelling difficulties and the lack of information about available options. This context propels the fear of failure and a lack of trust in entrepreneurial skills (OECD/EU, 2017[76]).

Policy insights

Policies to promote gender-neutral education and awareness of role models can play an important role to change society's perceptions about women's abilities as entrepreneurs. In addition to these pre-requirements, there is room for strengthening women's entrepreneurship even further in Chile by tackling the marital law, encouraging women to seek more external financing, and strengthening training programmes, including the mentoring and business development components of such programmes.

Step up the reform of the marital law by revamping the reform proposal that has been under discussion in Congress for the past eight years. As a minimum requirement, this would involve the abolition of the default rule, which foresees that the husband administers the marital property. The priority given to the most restrictive and disadvantageous option to women means that women have to pay a higher interest rate when applying for credit to launch a new business.

Encourage take-up of financing. Female entrepreneurs are less likely to seek funding to grow their business. A survey among entrepreneurs in Pacific Alliance countries found that male entrepreneurs are more likely to use each of the methods of financing mentioned by the questionnaire, including personal savings as the principal source, followed by friends and family; the financial system; public funds; business angels; investment funds and crowdfunding. Perhaps related to the impact of marital law, among Chilean micro-entrepreneurs, women seem less likely than men to seek a credit (Arellano and Peralta, 2016[77]), However, those who seek one seem to perceive public subsidies and access to private financing to be sufficient (OEAP, 2018[78]). It is unclear whether the same is true for entrepreneurs running small and medium enterprises.

The government should seek to maintain its good record of awarding funding to male and female entrepreneurs alike. It could also consider undertaking an in-depth study of the likelihood that male and female entrepreneurs obtain a funding tailored to their needs, taking into account their different personal and business characteristics. Finally, entrepreneurship-training courses for women could place more emphasis on when it makes sense to seek credit or other private or public-sector funding and how to go about obtaining it.

Enhance training programmes through long-term mentoring and business incubators. A review of existing programmes to support entrepreneurship in low- and middle-income countries confirms that training can play a powerful role in strengthening individuals' business competences with positive feedback effects on job creation. However, to be successful they have to meet certain requirements, such as targeting early entrepreneurs, being intensive and offered in combination with financial support (Grimm and Paffhausen, 2015[79]). Networking and mentoring guidance – via the creation of women's associations and forums, for example – are important catalysts of market information and can greatly facilitate knowledge sharing among peers.

These pre-conditions already apply to several of the Chilean programmes. Experience from European countries suggests that mentorship between experienced and new entrepreneurs can enhance business skills as well, if the mentor and mentee match well. Using interviews to figure out which mentor to match to which mentee is hence worthwhile. In addition, business accelerators or incubators can also provide opportunities for further training and networking in combination with business, financial and legal advice (OECD/EU, 2017[76]). Such accelerators could be run by the public sector itself or operated by the private or non-profit sector, with potential public funding (OECD/EU, 2019[80]).

Strengthening gender-sensitive approaches is essential to reach out to low income women. Work by the OECD shows that the adoption of gender-sensitive approaches in the design of training programmes is key to broadening access, thus expanding the pool of potentially interested women. Particularly, reaching out to women from low-income households requires the design of programmes that pay attention to certain day-to-day needs, such as women's time schedules, for example, and the need for assistance at home. This is important to secure continuity of care responsibilities, of the children and the elderly, during the time spent in training (OECD, 2019[81]).

Fighting violence against women

Mounting intolerance of violence against women during the past years has brought the fight against gender-based violence to the fore of the demand for increased social justice in Chile. This development is part of a pattern common to other Latin American countries. One prominent example is the action entailed by the #*Niunamenos* collective, which launched an awareness campaign, focusing on violence against women and the victims of femicide following the murder of a young Argentine woman. Mobilisations throughout the region, which has the highest rate of femicides in the world, increased after this campaign. Prompted by domestic developments and further spurred by regional movements, the Chilean authorities have taken initiatives to strengthen the laws against sexual harassment and gender-based violence (Red Chilena Contra las Violencias Hacia las Mujeres, 2020[82]). Law 20, 066, approved in 2010 defined femicide for the first time. It follows from the 1994 Law on Domestic Violence, which did not acknowledge that this crime has a strong gender component, despite the fact that over 80% of those attacked are women and over 80% of the aggressors are men. In 2020, the Gabriela Law (Law 21 212) expanded the definition of femicides to include attackers beyond current or former partners. In addition, the Ministry of Women and Gender Equality has promoted the launch of several awareness campaigns and broadcast through social networks and television channels, such as in 2018 the "Do not let it pass: Campaign against gender violence in Chile". The next section of this report provides a discussion of how the fight against gender-based violence has intensified during the COVID-19 crisis, including with the support of digital applications.

In addition to the laws against domestic violence, the Chilean legal system involves laws and regulations to combat harassment and violence against women in the public sphere. The 2012 Law No. 20 607 introduced sanctions against workplace harassment into the Chilean labor code. Schools and universities, in contrast, only have voluntary internal protocols for actions against school abuse, although cases can be reported to the Superintendence of Education if an institution does not take action. After almost two years of debate, the street sexual harassment law was unanimously approved in 2019. The penalties can range from 61 days to 5 years in prison with fines from USD 60 to USD 100 000.

Policy insights

Lower the barriers that prevent the victims of violence and harassment to access the justice system. Victims of violence against women often hesitate to report the crime for fear of high risks re-victimisation amid lengthy procedural requirements. Recent analysis of the issue suggests that on average, the processing time for sexual crimes in oral trials requires 947 days and fewer than 8% end with a conviction (Fiscalia de Chile, 2019[83]). Moreover, the Criminal Code defines rape and sexual abuse, narrowly implying that many practices considered as sexual violence are not recognised as crimes (OCAC, 2020[84]). Providing training to police and justice officers on how to address violence against women, including best practices on how to interact with the victims, can make the process of reporting these crimes less difficult. For example, in 2019, Mexico launched a police-training Programme that aims to ensure the correct application of procedural protocols in situations of gender violence. Hardly any victim can meet the current six-month deadline for reporting harassment or sexual violence, in particular against minors. Acknowledging the fact that the decision to report can be longer, a time extension seems desirable.

Encourage and guarantee safe complaint processes for victims. At workplaces, in schools and universities, women may be even more reluctant to report harassment or violence if the perpetrators are in a superior hierarchical position, such as teachers, supervisors or managers (ILO, 2018[85]). Accordingly, the Chilean Government could consider devoting more efforts to implementing safe complaint mechanisms to facilitate the reporting of these situations at the work place. International experience on the matter suggests that the policy initiatives to encourage companies to adopt complaint mechanisms can rely on different tools, such as collective agreements, for example, the regulations on Occupational Health and Safety and the employment legislation (Eurofound, 2015[86]). In the Scandinavian countries and the Netherlands, for example, the employers' obligation to set out procedures or measures to tackle violence and harassment in the workplace is a part of the approach to safeguard employees' mental and physical health. As such, it pertains to the regulations for improving well-being and health issues at work. Legislation in Belgium and France has introduced a specific duty on the employer to prevent violence and harassment. Ireland advices the employers to introduce a code of conduct in order to show their commitment to tackling abusive behaviour, which is highly relevant in case of a court claim.

The regulatory framework can also focus on prevention, setting out principles and guidelines to enable the employers adopting more pro-active initiatives. In compliance with these guidelines, some private employers have workshops and trainings in place to explain the law against sexual abuse at work and to raise awareness about the different manifestations of sexual abuse at work, along with how to report them. The role of social partners can also be important to scale up preventive actions at workplace level drawing from their expertise, including by helping the design of individual support, such as the presence of confidential counsellors.

Educate the youth about different aspects of sexual violence and harassment. Although Chile has launched awareness campaigns for sexual violence, these campaigns do not target teenagers, despite the fact that young women are often victims. One international example is the campaign #IlikeHowYouAre launched by Spain in 2019 to prevent gender violence among young people and targeting teenage girls and boys. Through the promotion of respect, acceptance and autonomy in the couple, the campaign focuses on the main manifestations of gender violence, with the aim of identifying and preventing them. A completely digitally supported campaign, it is disseminated through social networks. Other campaigns target street sexual harassment. In Argentina, the campaign #Cambiáeltrato, which showed a young man explaining to another that his behaviour with women on the street was not appropriate, went viral.

Monitor transport security. The lack of secure transports can lead women to restrict their movements as a way of reducing the exposure to risky behaviours. Such resolutions can discourage, in turn, women from participating in labour markets, with the adverse effects on incomes being potentially important for households in remote areas. In Chile, the 2018-22 Agenda for a Gender Equity Policy in Transport of the Ministry of Transport and Telecommunication defines goals to analyse the transport needs of women and to increase the security in public transport. While statistics on access to and security of transport and commuting characteristics for men and women exist for Santiago, similar information do not exist for rural areas, which limits the capacity to assess the effectiveness of policies (Duchène, 2011[87]).

Box 2.2. Summary of policy options for making women's paid work pay more in Chile

A range of concomitant policies can reduce the gender gap in labour income, thus contributing to lessening the incentive for women to spend more hours on unpaid work by. The OECD suggests to:

Ensure access to quality education for all

- *Provide additional support to vulnerable girls and teenage mothers.* Chile has made progress towards ensuring that teenage mothers stay in education and raising the impact of the policies to reduce premature pregnancies. In perspective, there could be scope for providing additional financial support to mothers and their young children as a way of ensuring that they can acquire basic education and skills that they can use at work.

- *Ensure comprehensive sexual education and information at school.* This requires guaranteeing a minimum curriculum on sexual and preventive education in every school and monitoring its implementation. A special advisor on health and sexual education inside schools could support students with appropriate information. It is advisable that the advisor be a trained young person, who the students can more easily identify as a peer, rather than a regular teacher.

- *Reward and communicate the benefits of completing studies.* Conditional cash transfers (CCTs) could provide a regular transfer benefits to parents of poor background who choose to keep their children at school. School mentoring, student counselling and targeted scholarships can be a key to helping girls and young women staying in education, if the mentors receive adapted training.

Promote women in non-traditional careers and leadership positions

- *Strengthen women's representation at the executive level in private sector companies.* The gender quota system has shown positive results in Chile's congress and state owned enterprises. However, the enforcement of a similar system or voluntary targets on boards and in senior management positions remains difficult among private sector companies.

- ***Step up monitoring and evaluation mechanisms with the aim to support the goal of equal pay for equivalent work.*** In Australia, the Workplace Gender Equality Act requires non-public sector employers with 100 or more employees to disclose their "Gender Equality Indicators" in annual filings submitted to the Workplace Gender Equality Agency.

- ***Step up efforts to raise girls' interest in science, technology and mathematics.*** Students should become aware of STEM before moving to post-secondary education so as to be able to make informed decisions about future careers. Mentorship programmes can allow them to identify positive role models, including by drawing inspiration from high-level positions in public and private companies. School textbooks could disseminate examples of male and female scientists. Public awareness campaigns can support the general fight against traditional gender stereotypes by showing that excelling in STEM areas is compatible with family life.

- ***Recognise and reinforce the application of statutory maternity and paternity leave in the academic sector and support access to care services.*** Expanding these rights, as proposed by a roadmap of the Ministry of Science for fostering the representation of women in science, can foster the attractiveness of academic careers to female science graduates. Mothers who return to work after their maternity leave should have the option to increase their working hours gradually.

Support female entrepreneurship

- ***Step up the reform of the marital law by revamping the proposal that has been under discussion in Congress for the past eight years.*** As a minimum requirement, this would necessitate the abolition of the default rule, which foresees that the husband administers the marital property.

- ***Continue to encourage take-up of financing.*** The government should seek to maintain its good record of awarding funding to male and female entrepreneurs alike. In addition, entrepreneurship training courses for women could place more emphasis on when it makes sense to seek credit or other private or public sector funding and how to go about obtaining it.

- ***Enhance training programmes through long-term mentoring and business incubators.*** Entrepreneurship training can play a powerful role in strengthening individuals' business skills and, potentially, job creation. However, to be successful they have to meet certain criteria, such as targeting early entrepreneurs, being intensive and offered in combination with financial support, networking and mentoring guidance – the creation of women's associations and forums, for example – are important catalysts of market information and can greatly facilitate knowledge sharing among peers.

- ***Strengthen gender-sensitive approaches is essential to reach out to low income women.*** Reaching out to women from low-income households requires the design of programmes that pay attention to certain day-to-day needs, such as women's time schedules, for example, and the need for assistance at home. This is important to secure continuity of care responsibilities of the children and the elderly during the time spent in training.

Fight violence against women

- ***Lower the barriers that prevent the victims of violence and harassment to access the justice system.*** Victims of violence against women often hesitate to report the crime for fear that lengthy procedural requirements will expose them to a high risk of re-victimisation. Moreover, the Criminal Code defines rape and sexual abuse, narrowly implying that many practices considered as sexual violence are not recognised as crimes. Providing training to police and justice officers on how to address violence against women, including best practices about how to interact with the victims, can make the process of reporting these crimes less difficult.

- **Encourage and guarantee safe complaint processes for victims.** At workplaces, in schools and universities, women may be reluctant to report harassment or violence if the perpetrators are in a superior hierarchical position, such as teachers, supervisors or managers. The Chilean Government could consider devoting more efforts to reinforce the implementation of safe complaint mechanisms capable of facilitating the reporting of these situations in the work place.

- **Educate the youth about different aspects of sexual violence and harassment.** Although Chile has launched awareness campaigns for sexual violence, they do not target teenagers, despite the fact that young women are most likely to be victims. An example of good practice is the Spanish campaign #IlikeHowYouAre, which was launched in 2019 to prevent gender violence among young people and is targeted to teenage girls and boys.

- **Monitor transport security.** The lack of secure transports can lead women to restrict their movements, hindering labour market participation. Further, take steps to strengthen the statistics of access to, and security of, transport and commuting conditions for men and women. While these statistics exist for Santiago, similar statistics do not exist for rural areas.

References

24 Horas (2020), "Cámara de Diputadas y Diputados despacha a ley proyecto "Crianza Segura"", *24 Horas*, https://www.24horas.cl/coronavirus/camara-de-diputadas-y-diputados-despacha-proyecto-crianza-segura-4336905. [20]

Albornoz Pollmann, L. (2017), *Women's Leadership in Latin America: The Key to Growth and Sustainable Development*, The Atlantic Council, Washington, D.C. [61]

Arellano, P. and S. Peralta (2016), *Emprendimiento y género: Cuarta Encuesta de Microemprendimiento*, Ministerio de Economía, Fomento y Turismo, https://www.economia.gob.cl/wp-content/uploads/2016/03/Informe-de-resultados-Emprendimiento-y-g%C3%A9nero.pdf. [77]

Bousseau, C. and P. Tap (1998), *Parental education and socialisation of the child: internality, valorisation and self-positioning*, https://halshs.archives-ouvertes.fr/halshs-01254469/document. [41]

Bünning, M. (2015), "What Happens after the 'Daddy Months'? Fathers' Involvement in Paid Work, Childcare, and Housework after Taking Parental Leave in Germany", *European Sociological Review*, Vol. 31/6, pp. 738-748, http://dx.doi.org/10.1093/esr/jcv072. [18]

Cámara de Diputadas y Diputados (2019), *A Sala proyecto que fortalece corresponsabilidad parental*, https://www.camara.cl/prensa/sala_de_prensa_detalle.aspx?prmid=138139. [22]

Chile Atiende (n.d.), *Programa 4 a 7, mujer trabaja tranquila*, https://www.chileatiende.gob.cl/fichas/12255-programa-4-a-7-mujer-trabaja-tranquila (accessed on 3 August 2020). [3]

Comunidad Mujer (2018), *Ranking Mujeres en la Alta Direccion 2018,* [68]
http://www.comunidadmujer.cl/biblioteca-publicaciones/wp-content/uploads/2019/01/Ranking-Mujeres-en-la-Alta-Direccio%CC%81n-2018.pdf.

CONICYT (2017), *Politica institucional de equidad de género en ciencia y tecnologia: Periodo* [70]
2017-2025, https://www.conicyt.cl/wp-content/uploads/2015/03/Politica-Institucional-Equidad-de-Genero-en-CyT-Periodo-2017_2025.pdf.

Cortázar, A. (2015), "Long-term effects of public early childhood education on academic [7]
achievement in Chile", *Early Childhood Research Quarterly*, Vol. 32, pp. 13-22,
https://doi.org/10.1016/j.ecresq.2015.01.003.

Council of Europe (2014), *Gender Stereotypes in and through education: Report of the 2nd* [52]
Conference of the Council of Euope National Focal Points on Gender Equality,
https://rm.coe.int/1680590fe5.

Council of Europe (2011), *Combating Gender Steroetypes in Education,* [54]
https://rm.coe.int/1680596131 (accessed on 20 January 2021).

Duchène, C. (2011), "Gender and Transport", *Discussion Paper*, No. 11, International Transport [87]
Forum, Paris.

ECLAC (2018), *Los cuidados en América Latina y el Caribe,* [2]
https://repositorio.cepal.org/bitstream/handle/11362/44361/1/S1801102_es.pdf (accessed on
23 March 2021).

EIGE (2020), *Gender mainstreaming: Ireland,* https://eige.europa.eu/gender-mainstreaming/countries/ireland (accessed on 20 January 2021). [55]

EU (2012), *Gender differences in educational outcomes: Study on the measures taken and the* [42]
current situation in Europe, https://op.europa.eu/en/publication-detail/-/publication/40271e21-ca1b-461e-ba23-88fe4d4b3fd4.

Eurofound (2015), *Violence and harassment in European workplaces: Extent, impacts and* [86]
policies, European Foundation for the Improvement of Living and Working Conditions, Dublin,
https://www.eurofound.europa.eu/sites/default/files/ef_comparative_analytical_report/field_ef_documents/ef1473en.pdf (accessed on 12 January 2021).

Fiscalia de Chile (2019), *Boletin III Trimsestre Enero-Septiembre 2020,* [83]
http://www.fiscaliadechile.cl/Fiscalia/estadisticas/index.do (accessed on 2 October 2020).

GOB (2020), *Proceso Constituyente: El 25 de octubre Chile decidió en las urnas,* [63]
https://www.gob.cl/procesoconstituyente/ (accessed on 28 October 2020).

Grimm, M. and A. Paffhausen (2015), "Do interventions targeted at micro-entrepreneurs and [79]
small and medium-sized firms create jobs? A systematic review of the evidence for low and
middle income countries", *Labour Economics*, Vol. 32, pp. 67-85,
https://doi.org/10.1016/j.labeco.2015.01.003.

Hagqvist, E. et al. (2017), "Parental leave policies and time use for mothers and fathers: a case [17]
study of Spain and Sweden", *Society, Health & Vulnerability*, doi:
10.1080/20021518.2017.1374103, p. 1374103,
http://dx.doi.org/10.1080/20021518.2017.1374103.

Hart, V. (2003), "Democratic Constitution Making", *United States Institute for Peace*, Vol. 107, https://www.usip.org/publications/2003/07/democratic-constitution-making. [67]

Heckman, J. et al. (2010), "The rate of return to the HighScope Perry Preschool Program", *Journal of Public Economics*, Vol. 94/1, pp. 114-128, https://doi.org/10.1016/j.jpubeco.2009.11.001. [6]

IDB (2015), "The Effect of Mandated Child Care on Female Wages in Chile", *National Bureau of Economic Research Working Paper Series*, Vol. No. 21080, https://publications.iadb.org/en/effect-mandated-child-care-female-wages-chile. [10]

IDEA (2019), "Women Constitution-Makers: Comparative Experiences with Representation, Participation and Influence", *First Annual Women Constitution-Makers'Dialogue, Edinburgh 2019*, https://www.idea.int/sites/default/files/publications/women-constitution-makers-comparative-experiences-with-representation-participation-influence.pdf (accessed on 28 October 2020). [66]

ILO (2020), *An employers' guide on working from home in response to the outbreak of COVID-19*, International Labour Organization, Geneva, https://www.ilo.org/wcmsp5/groups/public/---ed_dialogue/---act_emp/documents/publication/wcms_745024.pdf. [26]

ILO (2018), *Acabar con la violencia y el acoso contra las mujeres y los hombres en el mundo del trabajo*, https://www.ilo.org/wcmsp5/groups/public/---ed_norm/---relconf/documents/meetingdocument/wcms_554100.pdf. [85]

ILO (2018), *Garantizar un tiempo de trabajo decente para el futuro*, International Labour Organization, Geneva, https://www.ilo.org/wcmsp5/groups/public/---ed_norm/---relconf/documents/meetingdocument/wcms_618490.pdf. [24]

INE (2016), *Encuesta Nacional del Uso de Tiempo 2015 Cuadros Estadísticos*, https://www.ine.cl/estadisticas/sociales/genero/uso-del-tiempo (accessed on 3 August 2020). [1]

International Finance Corporation (2017), *Tackling Childcare - The Business Case for Employer-Supported Childcare*, International Finance Corporation, Washington, D.C., https://www.ifc.org/wps/wcm/connect/cd79e230-3ee2-46ae-adc5-e54d3d649f31/01817+WB+Childcare+Report_FinalWeb3.pdf?MOD=AJPERES&CVID=lXu9vP-. [12]

IPC-IG and UNICEF. (2020), *Maternidad y paternidad en el lugar de trabajo en América Latina y el Caribe — políticas para la licencia de maternidad y paternidad y apoyo a la lactancia materna*, entro Internacional de Políticas para el Crecimiento Inclusivo and UNICEF, Brasilia, https://uni.cf/2TSn1a6. [19]

IPI (2015), *Reimagining Peacemaking: Women's Roles in Peace Processes*, https://www.ipinst.org/wp-content/uploads/2015/06/IPI-E-pub-Reimagining-Peacemaking.pdf (accessed on 28 2020). [64]

Karlson and Simonsson (2011), *A question of Gender- Sensistive Pedagogy: discouses in pedagogical guidelines*, https://journals.sagepub.com/doi/pdf/10.2304/ciec.2011.12.3.274. [34]

Kotsadam, A. and H. Finseraas (2011), "The state intervenes in the battle of the sexes: Causal effects of paternity leave", *Social Science Research*, Vol. 40/6, pp. 1611-1622, https://doi.org/10.1016/j.ssresearch.2011.06.011. [16]

Kunze, A. (2018), "The Gender Wage Gap in Developed Countries", in Averett, S., L. Argys and S. Hoffman (eds.), *The Oxford Handbook of Women and the Economy*, Oxford University Press, Oxford, http://dx.doi.org/10.1093/oxfordhb/9780190628963.013.11. [37]

Lachance-Grzela, M. and G. Bouchard (2010), "Why Do Women Do the Lion's Share of Housework? A Decade of Research", *Sex Roles*, Vol. 63/11, pp. 767-780, http://dx.doi.org/10.1007/s11199-010-9797-z. [39]

Lexartza, L., M. Chaves and A. Cardeco (2016), *Policies to formalize paid domestic work in Latin America and the Caribbean*, Regional Office for Latin America and the Caribbean, Lima, https://www.ilo.org/wcmsp5/groups/public/---americas/---ro-lima/documents/publication/wcms_534457.pdf. [31]

Martínez A., C., E. Puentes and J. Ruiz-Tagle (2018), "The Effects of Micro-entrepreneurship Programs on Labor Market Performance: Experimental Evidence from Chile", *American Economic Journal: Applied Economics*, Vol. 10/2, http://dx.doi.org/10.1257/app.20150245. [75]

MINEDUC (2019), *Comision por una educacion con equidad de género: Propuestas de accion*, https://equidaddegenero.mineduc.cl/assets/pdf/propuestas-compressed.pdf. [50]

MINEDUC (2019), *http://convivenciaescolar.mineduc.cl/wp-content/uploads/2019/04/Protocolo-de-retenci%C3%B3n-en-el-sistema-escolar-de-estudiantes-embarazadas-madres-y-padres-adolescentes.-Mined.pdf*. [57]

MINEDUC (2019), *Minedu iniciará campaña para informar a padres de familia sobre el enfoque de género*, https://www.gob.pe/institucion/minedu/noticias/28286-minedu-iniciara-campana-para-informar-a-padres-de-familia-sobre-el-enfoque-de-genero. [53]

MINEDUC (2018), *Guias pedagogicas: eduquemos con igualdad*, https://www.mineduc.cl/wp-content/uploads/sites/19/2016/08/0.-Guias-pedagogicas-Campan%CC%83a-Eduquemos-con-Igualdad.pdf. [46]

MINEDUC (2018), *Indicadores de la Educacion en Chile: 2011-2016*, https://centroestudios.mineduc.cl/wp-content/uploads/sites/100/2018/03/INDICADORES_baja.pdf. [56]

MINEDUC (2016), *indicador Retención escolar*, https://www.curriculumnacional.cl/614/articles-90161_recurso_2.pdf. [58]

MINEDUC (2015), *Educar para la igualdad de género: Plan 2015-2018*, https://www.mineduc.cl/wp-content/uploads/sites/19/2017/01/CartillaUEG.pdf. [48]

Ministerio de Desarrollo Social y Família (n.d.), *Chile Cuida*, https://www.chilecuida.gob.cl/ (accessed on 3 August 2020). [4]

Ministerio del Interior y de la Seguridad Publica (2018), , https://www.diariooficial.interior.gob.cl/publicaciones/2018/02/10/41980/01/1351395.pdf. [49]

Moussié, R. (2016), *Child care from the perspective of women in the informal sector*, UN Secretary-General's High-Level Panel on Women's Economic Empowerment, https://www.wiego.org/sites/default/files/resources/files/WIEGO_childcare-informal-economy.pdf. [11]

Nores, M. and W. Barnett (2010), "Benefits of early childhood interventions across the world: (Under) Investing in the very young", *Economics of Education Review*, Vol. 29/2, pp. 271-282, https://doi.org/10.1016/j.econedurev.2009.09.001. [5]

Obrach King, Alexandra et al. (2017), *Salud sexual y reproductiva de adolescentes en Chile: el rol de la educacion sexual*, Revista Salud Publica, https://scielosp.org/pdf/rsap/2017.v19n6/848-854/es. [59]

OCAC (2020), *Radiografia del acoso sexual en Chile: Primera encuesta nacional sobre acoso sexual callejero, laboral, en*, https://www.ocac.cl/wp-content/uploads/2020/07/Informe-encuesta-OCAC-2020.-Radiograf%C3%ADa-del-acoso-sexual-en-Chile.pdf. [84]

OEAP (2018), *Brechas para el Emprendimiento en la Alianza del Pacífico*, Observatorio Estratégico de la Alianza del Pacífic, Santiago, http://centrodeinnovacion.uc.cl/assets/uploads/2018/12/estudio-brechas-para-el-emprendimiento-en-la-ap.pdf. [78]

OEAP (2018), *Programas de apoyo al Emprendimiento Feminino en la Alianza del Pacifico*, Observatorio Estratégico de la Alianza del Pacifico, https://asep.pe/wp-content/uploads/2018/11/Emprendimiento-Femenino-en-Latinoamerica-Informe-Mujeres-del-Pacifico.pdf. [74]

OECD (2020), *Iniciativa NiñaSTEM Pueden*, https://www.oecd.org/centrodemexico/iniciativa-niastem-pueden.htm (accessed on 2020). [72]

OECD (2020), "Productivity gains from teleworking in the post COVID-19 era : How can public policies make it happen?", *OECD Policy Responses to Coronavirus (COVID-19)*, OECD Publishing, Paris, https://doi.org/10.1787/a5d52e99-en. [32]

OECD (2020), *SIGI 2020 Regional Report for Latin America and the Caribbean*, Social Institutions and Gender Index, OECD Publishing, Paris, https://doi.org/10.1787/cb7d45d1-en. [73]

OECD (2019), *Corporate Governance Factbook 2019*, http://www.oecd.org/corporate/Corporate-Governance-Factbook.pdf. [71]

OECD (2019), *Enabling Women's Economic Empowerment: New Approaches to Unpaid Care Work in Developing Countries*, OECD Publishing, Paris, https://doi.org/10.1787/ec90d1b1-en. [81]

OECD (2019), *Prental Leave Systems*, https://www.oecd.org/els/soc/PF2_1_Parental_leave_systems.pdf (accessed on 23 March 2021). [29]

OECD (2018), *Enhancing Social Inclusion in Latin America: Key Issues and the Role of Social Protection Systems*, OECD, Paris, http://www.oecd.org/latin-america/regional-programme/Enhancing-Social-Inclusion-LAC.pdf. [30]

OECD (2017), *The Pursuit of Gender Equality: An Uphill Battle*, OECD Publishing, Paris, https://dx.doi.org/10.1787/9789264281318-en. [38]

OECD (2016), *Be Flexible! Background brief on how workplace flexibility can help European employees to balance work and family*, OECD, Paris, https://www.oecd.org/els/family/Be-Flexible-Backgrounder-Workplace-Flexibility.pdf. [28]

OECD (2015), *The ABC of Gender Equality in Education: Aptitude, Behaviour, Confidence*, PISA, OECD Publishing, Paris, https://dx.doi.org/10.1787/9789264229945-en.   [36]

OECD (2012), *Closing the Gender Gap: Act Now*, OECD Publishing, Paris, https://dx.doi.org/10.1787/9789264179370-en.   [33]

OECD (n.d.), *OECD Family Database*, http://www.oecd.org/social/family/database.htm.   [23]

OECD/EU (2019), *Policy Brief on Incubators and Accelerators that Support Inclusive Entrepreneurship*, Publications Office of the European Union, Luxembourg, http://dx.doi.org/10.2767/092345.   [80]

OECD/EU (2017), *Policy Brief on Women's Entrepreneurship*, Publications Office of the European Union, Luxembourg, https://www.oecd.org/cfe/smes/Policy-Brief-on-Women-s-Entrepreneurship.pdf.   [76]

OXFAM (2007), *Practicing Gender Euqality in Education*, https://oxfamilibrary.openrepository.com/bitstream/handle/10546/115528/bk-practising-gender-equality-education-150607-en.pdf?sequence=5.   [44]

OXFAM (2005), *Gender Equality in Schools*, http://www.ungei.org/oxfam_edPaper2.pdf.   [43]

Red Chilena Contra las Violencias Hacia las Mujeres (2020), *Violencia contra mujeres en Chile: dossier informativo 2019-2020*, http://www.nomasviolenciacontramujeres.cl/wp-content/uploads/2020/08/dossier-red-corre.pdf.   [82]

Rhee, J., N. Done and G. Anderson (2015), "Considering long-term care insurance for middle-income countries: comparing South Korea with Japan and Germany", *Health Policy*, Vol. 119/10, pp. 1319-1329, https://doi.org/10.1016/j.healthpol.2015.06.001.   [14]

Rich, M. (2019), "Two Men in Japan Dared to Take Paternity Leave. It Cost Them Dearly, They Say", *New York Times*, https://www.nytimes.com/2019/09/12/world/asia/japan-paternity-leave.html.   [21]

Scholarship, O. (ed.) (1998), *The Politics of Presence*, Oxford Scholarship, http://dx.doi.org/DOI:10.1093/0198294158.001.0001.   [65]

Senado (2019), *Logran histórico acuerdo para Nueva Constitución: participación ciudadana será clave*, https://www.senado.cl/logran-historico-acuerdo-para-nueva-constitucion-participacion/senado/2019-11-14/134609.html (accessed on 28 October 2020).   [62]

SENAMA (2013), *Maltrato Contra las Personas Mayores:Una Mirada desde la Realidad Chilena*, Ministerio de Desarrollo Social, Santiago, http://www.flacsochile.org/wp-content/uploads/2013/11/SENAMA-Cuadernillo3-CAMBIOS-6-de-noviembre-2013.pdf.   [8]

SERNAM (2009), "Analisis de género en el aula", *Documento de Trabajo* 117.   [45]

Sistema de Empresas (2016), *Presencia femenina en directorios de empresas públicas bordeó el 30% en 2015*, http://www.sepchile.cl/prensa/noticias/noticias/?no_cache=1&tx_ttnews%5Btt_news%5D=438&cHash=2d08f9e4637af522a70fc23c91a5906a (accessed on 12 January 2021).   [69]

Soto, T. et al. (2018), *Teletrabajo en el Estado de Chile: Efectos y desafíos para su diseño e implementación*, Centro de Sistemas Públicos (CSP), Ingeniería Industrial, Universidad de Chile, http://www.trendtic.cl/wp-content/uploads/2018/10/CSP-SSP16-Teletrabajo-en-el-Estado-de-Chile-1.pdf. [27]

Thévenon, O. and A. Solaz (2013), "Labour Market Effects of Parental Leave Policies in OECD Countries", *OECD Social, Employment and Migration Working Papers*, No. 141, OECD Publishing, Paris, https://dx.doi.org/10.1787/5k8xb6hw1wjf-en. [15]

UDP (2018), *Informe anual sobre derechos humanos en Chile 2018*, http://www.derechoshumanos.udp.cl/derechoshumanos/images/InformeAnual/2018/Muoz-y-Ramos-Educacin-y-Genero.pdf. [47]

UN Women (2017), *Long-term Care for Older People - A New Gender Policy Priority*, UN Women, New York, https://www.unwomen.org/-/media/headquarters/attachments/sections/library/publications/2017/un-women-policy-brief-09-long-term-care-for-older-people-en.pdf?la=en&vs=1608. [13]

UNESCO (2018), *International Technical Guidance on Sexuality Education, an Evidence Informed approach*, OECD, Paris, http://unesdoc.unesco.org/images/0026/002607/260770e.pdf. (accessed on 12 January 2021). [60]

UNESCO (2017), *Una mirada a la profesion docente en el Peru: Futuros docentes, docentes en servicio y formadores docentes*, https://unesdoc.unesco.org/ark:/48223/pf0000260917/PDF/260917spa.pdf.multi. [51]

UNESCO (2004), *Gender sensitivity: a training manual for sensitizing education managers, curriculum and material developers and media professionals to gender concerns*, https://unesdoc.unesco.org/ark:/48223/pf0000137604_eng. [40]

Wahlstrom, K. (2003), *Flickor pojkar och pedagoger [Girls, boys and pedagogues]*. [35]

Yañez, S. (2016), *¿Tiempo de Trabajo Decente? La jornada laboral en América Latina e instrumentos y mecanismos de su flexibilización*, FLACSO, Santiago, http://www.flacsochile.org/wp-content/uploads/2016/09/Doc-Trabajo-N%C2%BA1-Tiempo-de-trabajo-decente_opt.pdf. [25]

Yévenes, P. (2018), "La sala cuna universal en 10 preguntas", https://www.latercera.com/nacional/noticia/la-sala-cuna-universal-10-preguntas/274976/. [9]

3 The compounding effects of COVID-19

This chapter provides a detailed overview of the health social and economic well-being impacts of the COVID-19 pandemic in Chile. It finds that COVID-19 and the lockdown have dramatically exacerbated gender inequalities at least temporarily. The chapter starts with a review of labour market developments. The pandemic has exacerbated the main breadwinner role of men. Conversely, Chilean women who stopped working did not search for re-employment because they took on additional caring work. In addition to higher labour market inactivity, the pandemic also led to an exacerbation of stress and mental health problems and an upsurge of episodes of violence against women. The chapter then reviews the early steps that the Chilean Government has taken to mitigate these adverse consequences and advances a set of policy insights for continued government efforts to support women, particularly the most vulnerable.

On 8 March 2020, just before countries throughout the world introduced lockdown measures in response to the COVID-19 outbreak, thousands of Chilean women of different ages and backgrounds took part in a Women's Day march that many commentators designated as historical. What made this march unique was a sentiment that Chile was right at a turning point in the fight for gender equality and that the soon to come constitutional referendum would open the way to a brighter future of stronger female representation and equality in law-making (Escobar, 2020[1]). The referendum's adoption establishing that half of the members of the constitutional convention will be women supported the general confidence in the role that Chilean women can play as actors for change. The approach is indeed unprecedented, making Chile the first country to write its constitution under conditions of gender parity.

However, the labour market and well-being situation of Chilean women has deteriorated dramatically since the onset of the pandemic, leading to the exacerbation of stress and mental health problems and to an upsurge of episodes of violence against women. These sudden developments have brought to light, in an unprecedented way, a number of fundamental pre-existing challenges and that there is still a way to go before the policies to account for gender inequalities in Chile meet women's unique needs, responsibilities and perspectives.

This chapter provides a detailed overview of the health, social and economic well-being impacts of the COVID-19 pandemic in Chile. It finds that the COVID-19 and the lockdown have dramatically exacerbated gender inequalities and reviews the early steps that the Chilean Government has taken to mitigate these consequences.

Women and COVID-19 in Chile: Review of impacts and challenges

The pandemic hit Chile hard, with the country suffering one of the highest numbers of deaths per million inhabitants (OECD, 2020[2]). Most cases are concentrated in the Santiago metropolitan area, with scattered outbreaks in other regions of the country. The government responded by applying local quarantine requirements, combined with mobility restrictions and night curfews. By May 2020, the city of Santiago and other large cities were under a strict lockdown, with most containment measures lifted progressively in mid-July, when infections started declining. A state of emergency, declared in March to impose containment measures, lasted until the end of 2020.

Labour market developments

The *status quo ante* in Chile was one whereby only about 50% of women participated in the labour market before the pandemic, compared with 70% of men (Figure 1.6, Chapter 1). Following the outbreak of the COVID-19 crisis, Chile recorded a sharp drop in employment rates during the first half of 2020, in excess of 10 percentage points among both men and women. Since the respective rates fell by approximately the same extent, the crisis hit male and female workers to similar degrees (Figure 3.1). One reason for this resemblance is that the most-hit sectors include those in which women are over-represented, such as retail and hotel and food services, as well as those where men are over-represented, such as construction (INE, 2020[3]).

Figure 3.1. The employment-to-population ratio of Chilean women fell by a quarter between January and June 2020

Employment-to-population ratio of 15-64 year-olds

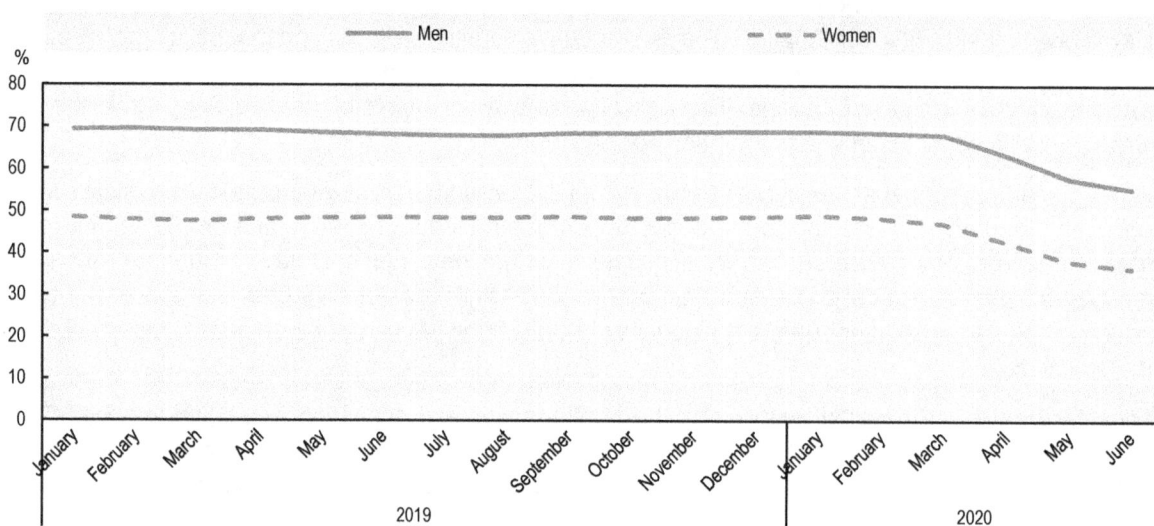

Note: The statistics refer to rolling quarterly figures. For example, the value for June 2020 refers to the average for April to June 2020.
Source: Instituto Nacional de Estadistica (2020[4]), *Banco de datos de la Encuesta Nacional de Empleo*, http://bancodatosene.ine.cl/.

Figure 3.2 compares the fall in employment across 12 Latin American and Caribbean countries with available data. In Chile, the employment rate fell by a larger extent than the regional average (Panel A). Importantly, many employees who lost their job did not search for a new one, either because they believed the probability of finding one was too low given the restrictions imposed on economic activities, or out of caution regarding the risk of infection (ECLAC and ILO, 2020[5]). For example, many self-employed people decided to wait for better conditions before resuming their activities. As these workers abandoned the labour market, they no longer met the requirements for unemployment classification – i.e. they became inactive – and accordingly, the fall in employment resulted in a sharp contraction of participation rates. The extent of the combined contraction between men and women approximates 10 percentage points in Chile, which compares with 8 percentage points for the average of the regional countries with available data (Figure 3.2, Panel B).

Figure 3.2. Labour market developments in the aftermath of the pandemic

Year-on-year changes using differences between second quarter rates of 2020 and 2019, in percentage points

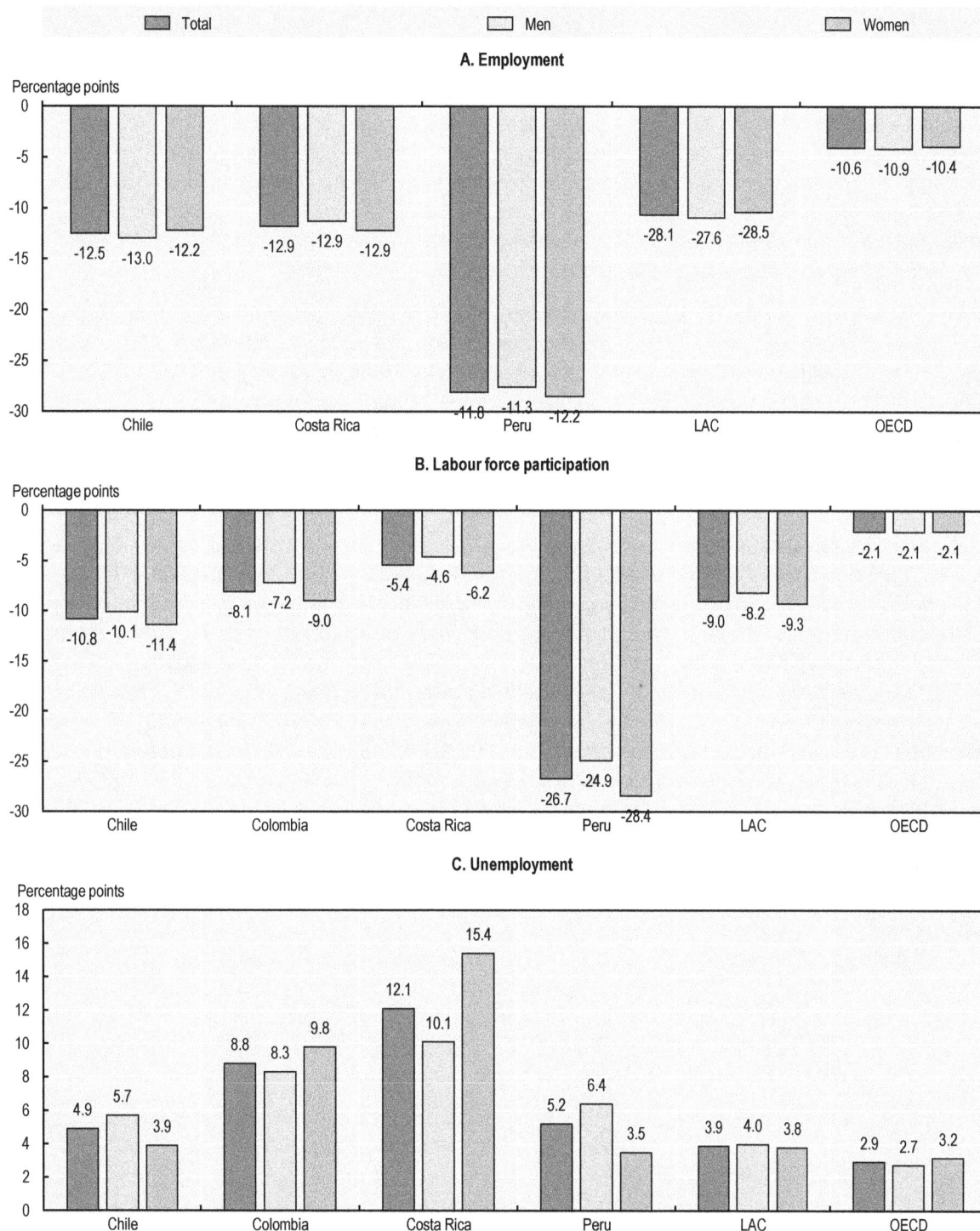

Note: LAC simple average of 12 countries: Argentina, Bolivia, Brazil, Chile, Colombia, Costa Rica, the Dominican Republic, Ecuador, Mexico, Paraguay, Peru and Uruguay.
Source: OECD: http://dotstat.oecd.org//Index.aspx?QueryId=103557; LAC: Economic Commission for Latin America and the Caribbean (ECLAC)/C)/International Labour Organization (ILO), "Employment trends in an unprecedented crisis: policy challenges", Employment Situation in Latin America and the Caribbean, No. 23 (LC/TS.2020/128), Santiago, 2020.

For the average of the LAC countries listed above, the massive fall of labour market participation rates mitigated, in turn, the impact on the unemployment rate. In Chile, however, the extent of the increase of the unemployment rate amongst men was almost 2 percentage points bigger than observed in the average of the LAC countries (+5.7%, compared to +4.0%; Figure 3.2, Panel C). This contrasts starkly with the increase of the unemployment rate amongst women, which in Chile remained well aligned to the regional average (+3.9%, compared to +3.8%).

Gender differences in unemployment patterns mask important differences in the way Chilean men and women have responded to the pandemic. Particularly, it seems likely that the role that men play as the main breadwinners of the household strengthened even more in the aftermath of the pandemic. Accordingly, the marked increase of the male unemployment rate reflects the fact that they have continued to look for new jobs (ECLAC and ILO, 2020[5]). Other regional countries have behaved similarly, but the stronger than average increase of the male unemployment rate in Chile suggests that the "men as breadwinner" effect could have been particularly pronounced in the country.

Conversely, as many as 80% of all Chilean women who stopped working during the pandemic did not search for re-employment – with 30% of these women being the head of household in 2020 (Escobar, 2020[1]). This large withdrawal of women from the labour market is the mirror image of the fact that women assumed additional caring work during the pandemic. If the women's unemployment rate increased less than that of men, it was because they stopped actively looking for a new job in the paid labour market.

Low-income women

The high inactivity rates experienced by women workers have likely led to substantial losses of households' incomes. To help to shine a light on this particular issue, Figure 3.3 depicts the evolution of female head of households in Chile, measured as the percentage share of the total number of households over a period of almost three decades. It shows that this share underwent a significant increase during the period, particularly dramatic since the turn of the century, from 23.2% of all country's households in 2000 to 42.4% in 2017. At the same time, the structure of households also changed significantly in Chile, with single households having almost doubled (from 8.7% of total households in 2006 to 15.4% in 2017). During the same period, two-parent households decreased from 67.6% to 56.6%, while single-parent households increased by 3 percentage points, reaching 27.4%. Recent analysis shows that, during the pandemic, 52% of low-income women in Chile (first income decile) were unable to work reflecting the pandemic, which is 5 percentage points higher than observed for low-income men (Gutierrez, Martin and Nopo, 2020[6]).

Figure 3.3. Evolution of households headed by women in Chile

Percentage shares of total households

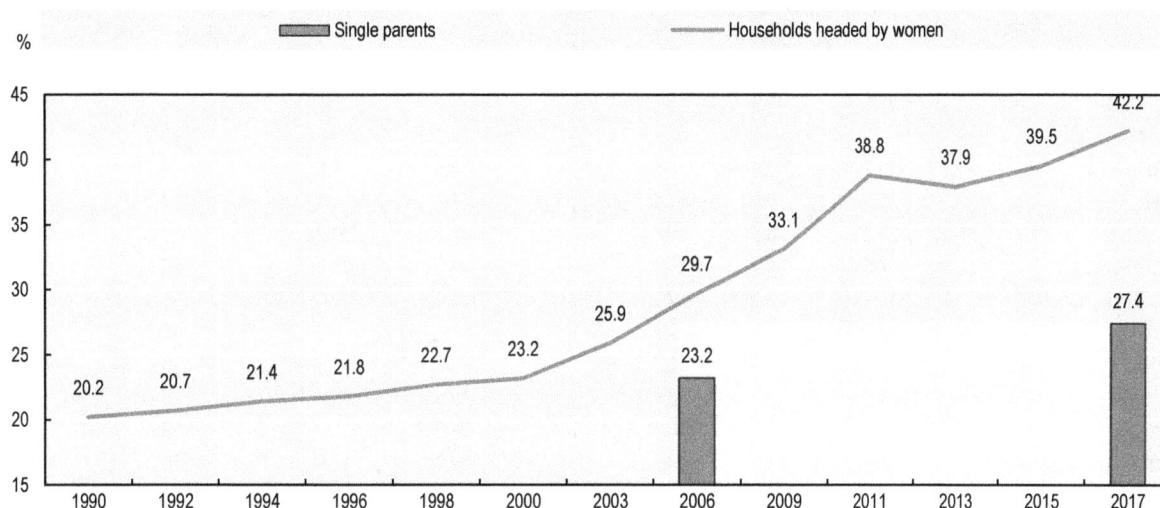

Source: Ministerio de Desarrollo Social y Familia, Encuesta Casen 1990-2017.

Table 3.1 illustrates the effects of the COVID-19 pandemic on specific occupational categories. It highlights that the health crisis hit particularly strongly work categories that are typically characterised by the over-representation of women workers from low-income households. It is revealing, for example, that the number of dependent employed people working in households as care or house workers fell by almost 48% in Chile during the second quarter of 2020. This contraction was significantly stronger than experienced by the average of Latin America countries with available figures (32%).

Another category that deserves mention is own-account work/self-employment. As foreshadowed during the discussion about women's labour market developments in Chile, this is an important source of female work in the country. Employment in this category contracted by close to 35% in Chile, which compares with a regional average of about 21%. Many own-account activities rely on face-to-face contact relations, especially when they occur in the informal sector, and are therefore not adapted to teleworking. This meant that distancing measures resulted in their interruption (ECLAC and ILO, 2020[5]).

Possibly related to the sharp contraction in own-account work, Chile also underwent a considerable decline in the number of people carrying out unpaid work activities in the context of a family-owned business. As often happens, these are own-account activities, with women the main carriers. Across the Latin American countries unpaid workers constitute the second most affected category by the pandemic – after wage earners working in households – with the related contraction having averaged 24.2%. In Chile, the fall of unpaid workers was significantly stronger than the regional average (42%). One explanation of the more marked contraction of own-account and unpaid workers in Chile than other regional comparators (Colombia, Ecuador, Paraguay and Bolivia, for example), could be that in the latter countries own-account workers continue to account for a significant part of the agricultural sector. These activities are likely to have suffered less the introduction of containment measures (ECLAC and ILO, 2020[5]).

Table 3.1. Employment patterns by occupational categories in selected Latin American countries

Year-on-year percentage changes of employed persons, second quarter of 2020

	Wage earners in companies and institutions			Wage earners in households	Employers	Own-Account workers	Unpaid workers
	Private	Public	Total				
Argentina	-21.1	+8.9	-15.6	-38.2	-39.5	-28.2	-7.8
Bolivia	...	...	-17.4	-26.6	-39.8	+0.3	-8.0
Brazil	-13.2	+6.0	-9.3	-24.6	-9.5	-10.3	-15.5
Chile	-15.5	-0.6	-12.9	-47.7	-34.6	-34.7	-41.7
Colombia	-24.2	-3.6	-22.6	-44.7	-30.2	-17.9	-29.1
Costa Rica	-17.5	-4.4	-14.8	-44.0	-33.8	-25.1	-27.9
Dominican Republic	-11.2	+3.9	-7.3	-31.1	-9.4	-6.8	-23.2
Ecuador	-19.7	-5.6	-17.5	...	...	-10.2	-31.2
Mexico	-13.6	+4.0	-12.5	...	-17.5	-30.9	-35.7
Paraguay	-11.7	+2.2	-8.7	-15.5	-48.4	+12.7	+5.0
Peru	...	...	-48.3	-68.8	...	-63.4	-69.0
Latin America, weighted average	-14.7	+4.2	-14.2	-32.2	-17.9	-20.5	-24.3
Latin America, Median	-15.5	+2.2	-14.8	-38.2	-33.8	-17.9	-2.0

Source: OECD: http://dotstat.oecd.org//Index.aspx?QueryId=103557; LAC: Economic Commission for Latin America and the Caribbean (ECLAC)/C)/International Labour Organization (ILO), "Employment trends in an unprecedented crisis: policy challenges", Employment Situation in Latin America and the Caribbean, No. 23 (LC/TS.2020/128), Santiago, 2020.

Unpaid caring responsibilities

Confinement and social distancing measures have led to an abrupt reduction not only of formal care activities by childcare and education centres, but also informal care arrangements to support families and neighbours (Women, UN; ECLAC;, 2020[7]). In mid-March, the Chilean Government decided to close schools, with the Ministry of Education implementing new measures focussed on virtual-learning, to allow students to continue their school programmes from home. The *Aprendo en Línea* platform gives students and teachers access to a variety of on-line learning materials and pedagogical tools, as part of the prioritised school curriculum adopted in response to the crisis (MINEDUC, 2020[8]). Moreover, new educational television programmes are now in use to support teachers and parents in the organisation of home-schooling activities.

However, limited access to the internet implies that distance learning is more difficult for many Chilean students, particularly those from low-income households, who are less connected, or whose parents are unable to help them. In Chile, although only 12% of households indicate that they have no access to the internet, the proportion of those who have a stable connection remains small (46%) (Brújula, 2017[9]). Among children from poor families, the proportion of those who have adequate access to the internet – i.e. enough stable to allow them following school from home – is even smaller (30%) (Escobar, 2020[1]).

Given that the health system operated at maximum capacity during the pandemic, much of the health care burden shifted to households. This exacerbated the complexity of the organisation of health care and the core role that women played in the care of family members' health even more (ECLAC, 2020[10]). A recent survey by the Ministry of Social Development shows that in Chile 70% of care-dependent older people receive help from family members to carry out activities of daily living, with women representing 72% of caregivers (Ministerio de Desarrollo Social, 2017[11]). These activities involve, among other tasks, purchasing medicines, engaging services and providing direct care for sick people. Out of the total number of care-dependent older people who receive assistance from outside the family, only 10% remunerate the caregiver. In addition, 71% of Chilean men dedicated zero hours to domestic and parental work during the week of realisation of the survey in July 2020 (Escobar, 2020[1]).

Overall, the combination of temporary closure of care and education centres with the extra pressure on the health systems, significantly added to the time already spent by women on chore activities at home. This led to exacerbate an already unbalanced allocation of paid and unpaid work activities between men and women within the family. According to a recent survey jointly launched in Chile by the Ministry of Women and Gender Equality and UN Women to assess the effects of COVID-19, half of women declared that the time doing unpaid care and domestic work increased significantly (MinMujEG, 2021[12]).

Mental health

Changes in routines, forced isolation and the anxiety of losing income have resulted in stress and fear. A survey by the University of Chile (University of Chile and IMIIMPP, 2020[13]) argues that living in the pandemic crisis has involved a mix of generational and gender consequences. The proportion of people expressing concern about the economic effects of the crisis is higher among the young generations (in the 15-29 years age bracket) than among older age groups. The perception that well-being and mental health conditions are getting worse is also more widespread among the young. These sentiments appear to be more common among women and manifest in fatigue, feelings of sadness and distress. The findings of the University of Chile corroborate the results of another survey that UNICEF has carried out in nine Latin America and Caribbean countries. According to the latter, 27% of young people aged between 13 and 29 reported a sense of anxiety during the seven days prior to the survey and 15% a feeling of depression (UNICEF, 2020[14]). One possible explanation of the observed differences between age and gender effects relates to the fact that, for many girls, the halting of classes at schools and universities has meant a rise in the time spent on the care of their siblings.

Domestic violence

Although confinement measures helped to keep people safe from the virus, for women they inadvertently widened the exposure to other risks (OEA, 2020[15]; PAHO, 2020[16]; UN WOMEN, 2020[17]). Adding to the stress induced by a heavier workload at home, one prominent risk stems from the danger of domestic violence (UNDP, 2020[18]). In Latin America and the Caribbean, where gender-based violence was already widespread prior to the pandemic, this issue is particularly concerning.

While data from sources such as police reports, helplines, health centres, and shelters provide essential insights, they are unlikely to reflect the true situation, since the victims of violence often do not report episodes for reasons relating to shame, stigma, or fear of retaliation. This under-reporting may be even greater during the pandemic, since mobility restrictions and fear of contagion may hinder the capacity to seek help in person. Telephone or internet reporting may also be limited, given that victims have fewer opportunities to reach out secretly when confined at home with their abuser.

These caveats withstanding, the UNDP has collected data on calls to helplines in a selected number of Latin American countries – Argentina (Línea 137 in Buenos Aires and Línea 144), Brazil (Ligue 180), Colombia (Línea 155), Guatemala (Línea 1 572), Mexico (Línea Mujeres in Mexico City), Paraguay (Línea 137), and Peru (Línea 100 and Chat 100). In all these countries, the volume of calls to helplines has increased following the introduction of mobility restrictions. These patterns appear supported by emerging evidence from other regional studies using helpline data for several countries (UNDP, 2020[18]). Evidence gathered by Infosegura, which regularly collects data on citizen security in Central American countries, shows increased levels of gender-based violence in Guatemala, El Salvador, Honduras and Costa Rica during the first trimester of 2020 (Infoseguras, 2020[19]).

In Chile, calls made to "1455", the hotline of the National Service of Women and Gender Equality, have increased by 229% between March and June (Fernandez and Lopez, 2020[20]). Data from the National

Service of Women and Gender Equality (SernamEG) for the period January to May shows a similarly sharp increase (Gandara, 2020[21]) The police reported an increase of 119% in calls regarding physical intra-family violence against women during the four weeks that followed the introduction of mobility restrictions (149 assistance number) (MINMUJERyEG, 2020[22]). However, the formal filing of legal denunciations has decreased (CEAD, 2020[23]). Since the restrictions have made the police stations less accessible to victims than help centres, this evidence may only be indicative of reduced reporting through the legal channel, rather than pointing to a reduction in violence.

Gender sensitive policy responses to support economic security

Measures to support SMEs and employment

The Chilean Government has introduced numerous gender sensitive policy responses to counter the economics and social effects of the pandemic (OECD, 2020[2]). The measures most likely to have supported women's economic security included a focus on entrepreneurship and loan subsidies. One key initiative consisted of the launch of a USD 5.5 billion emergency package to save jobs and help small businesses. As a complement to this, the government also decided to defer various taxes on SMEs and to accelerate the income tax refund for SMEs (to April 2020 instead of May, which is set to benefit 500.000 small companies). In addition, the capital of the guarantee fund for SMEs (Fogape) was increased by USD 3 000 million, with 150 000 loans granted by the beginning of July. In parallel, the increased capitalisation of *Banco Estado* (by USD 500 million, leading the Banco's credit capacity to increase by USD 4.4 billion) should result in more financing opportunities to individuals and SMEs.

One key measure to tackle the large increase of labour market inactivity has been the concession of a temporary hiring subsidy to companies, which applies to all new employees and primarily the expansion of women employment. The subsidy extends over a period of six months, covering 60% and 50% of the gross salary for each women hire and men hire, respectively. In order for the hiring subsidy to trigger more job searches by women, it needs the support of certain complementary measures, such as those aimed at securing the safe return of children to educational establishments. It also needs the support of measures to extend access to digital services, from virtual trainings and financial education, to home delivery and marketing platforms.

Facilitating more flexible work hours and arrangements is another policy option. The COVID-19 has played a role in accelerating the adoption of the Act on Distance Work and Teleworking to broaden the use of teleworking. In addition, the Act for the Protection of Work aims at protecting labour incomes and reducing working hours, or allowing for the temporary suspension of the contractual relationship when teleworking is not possible. In the latter cases, the unemployment insurance intervenes to protect the salaries of concerned workers, while also ensuring the continuation of social security and health contributions.

Protecting incomes

A range of measures falls into the social protection category. A special subsidy (COVID bonus) targets 1.5 million vulnerable households, most of them without formal income. The programme *Alimentos para Chile* (Food for Chile) provides food baskets and hygiene products to vulnerable and middle-class families across Chilean regions. A new fund to protect the income of the 80% most vulnerable households aims to provide cash transfers to vulnerable households (Emergency Family Income). It should reach out to 4.9 million beneficiaries, depending on personal circumstances, including by providing support to independent workers.

In July 2020 and in response to the COVID-19 pandemic, Chile enacted measures for parents on parental leave and for parents and caregivers of children born in or after 2013 (i.e. seven years of age or younger). The law provides parents with an extension of up to 90 days of additional parental leave benefits and allows eligible parents and caregivers to suspend their employment contract with employers in order to provide childcare and receive unemployment benefits. Furthermore, 240 000 primary and lower secondary students in isolated areas received learning materials, and students who would normally qualify for free breakfast and lunch at school are entitled to receive food packages (MINEDUC, 2020[8]).

The fight against gender-based violence

A number of measures focus on preventing and/or responding to violence against women and girls, with the Ministry of Women and Gender Equality playing a leading role in efforts to strengthen the digital networks available to the victims of domestic violence (OECD, 2020[24]). April 2020 saw the launch of two platforms aimed at providing help to women who are victims and survivors of violence, "Chat 1455" and "WhatsApp Mujer" (WhatsApp for Women), the latter provided by the National Service for Women and Gender Equity (SernamEG). Both platforms are available 24/7 and are confidential, with the objective of providing information, guidance, and emotional support to victims of violence. In May, the Ministry of Women and Gender Equality announced a third initiative, *Mascarilla 19* (Facemask 19), which is a code word that women can use in pharmacies to report a dangerous home situation without having to call the police, which could risk alerting the abuser. If a woman asks for a *Mascarilla 19*, the pharmacy staff know it is a case of violence and will proceed to write down the victim's details and pass the information on to Chat 1455, or the police.

Supportive dissemination campaigns ensure that people are aware of the existence of the services so that women in need feel encouraged to call for guidance. These campaigns rely on television broadcasts but also, and predominantly, on social networks, which significantly limits the capacity to reach out to the areas least equipped with fixed internet connection. Coincidentally, these are also the places known for having the highest rates of domestic violence within the Santiago Metropolitan area – La Pintana, Cerro Navia, Lo Prado, La Granja, Renca and San Ramón.

In addition to orientation services, SernamEG's protection programmes for victims of domestic violence encompass 111 nationwide Women's Centres, which provide legal advice and psychological support to women in situations of violence. They also include 44 Shelters in the country, which receive women in situations of risk and extreme violence. Although the approved and budgeted construction of four additional shelters dates to prior to the onset of the pandemic, the actual construction remains pending.

Policy insights

The COVID-19 pandemic has uncovered the extent of existing labour market and well-being challenges facing Chilean women. The outbreak of the pandemic has led to higher labour market inactivity, associated with an exacerbation of stress and mental health problems and an upsurge of episodes of violence against women.

The significant increase in labour market inactivity heightens the importance of continued government efforts to support the most vulnerable women. Even before the pandemic, only about 50% of women participated in the Chilean labour market, compared with 70% of men. Compounding this situation, the closure of early childcare institutions and schools, in combination with the increased vulnerability of the elderly, led to a surge in the demand for care within the households, at a point in time when the health system was operating at maximum capacity. The evidence of large increases in inactivity underscores the importance to facilitate access to benefits targeted at low-income families – in particular single parents, who are predominantly female – and targeted programmes to support women's return to employment.

Provide support to gender-sensitive measures that can help prevent inactivity from increasing further. This includes actively informing firms about how to reduce working hours, provide relief for workers, and manage redundancy payments related to temporary lay-offs and sick leave. Importantly, it also includes ensuring that the self-employed can access emergency measures, especially those who do not qualify for employment insurance. The effects of more forward looking support measures with a potential to strengthen the resilience of women's employment and support gender equality in the future, deserve close assessment. This includes by monitoring the outcomes of the adoption of the Act on Distant Work and Teleworking and of the new measures for employees on parental leave.

Consider authorising local re-openings of education institutions, based on the assessment of area-specific infection conditions. By allowing families in the least affected areas to put their children back into in-person education, targeted openings would encourage more women to actively search for a job, thus countering the rise of labour market inactivity, which is a first priority. In addition, targeted openings could help to alleviate the financial grief suffered by many education establishments during the school closures.[1]

Continue efforts to push back on social acceptance of domestic violence by drawing attention to how the issue affects women in confinement. The important actions to foster the introduction of more electronically-based modes of communication should be complemented by measures to ensure that service delivery for victims is integrated across relevant spheres so that all public agencies engaged in this issue work in a closely co-ordinated manner and ensure that timely access to justice is strengthened during the crisis. These include the spheres of health, social services, education, employment and justice.

More fundamentally, all of the above economic and social policy measures must be embedded in broader efforts to mainstream gender in governments' responses to the crisis. In the short term, it means, wherever possible, applying a gender lens to emergency policy measures. In the longer term, it means that the government implements a well-functioning system of gender mainstreaming, relying on ready access to gender-disaggregated evidence in all sectors so that differential effects on women and men can be readily assessed.

References

Brújula (2017), *IX Encuesta de Acceso y Usos de Internet*, Subsecretaría de Telecomunicaciones de Chile , Santiago, https://www.subtel.gob.cl/wp-content/uploads/2018/07/Informe_Final_IX_Encuesta_Acceso_y_Usos_Internet_2017.pdf. [9]

CEAD (2020), *Informe de Resultados IV Encuesta de Violencia contra la Mujer en el Ámbito de Violencia Intrafamiliar y en Otros Espacios (ENVIF-VCM)*, http://cead.spd.gov.cl/centro-de-documentacion/. [23]

ECLAC (2020), *The COVID-19 pandemic is exacerbating the care crisis in Latin America and the Caribbean*, https://repositorio.cepal.org/bitstream/handle/11362/45352/4/S2000260_en.pdf (accessed on 25 January 2021). [10]

ECLAC and ILO (2020), *Employment Situation in Latin America and the Caribbean. Employment trends in an unprecedented crisis: policy challenges*, https://www.cepal.org/en/publications/46309-employment-situation-latin-america-and-caribbean-employment-trends-unprecedented (accessed on 25 January 2021). [5]

Escobar, P. (2020), "Coronavirus & Gender: The Other Pandemic in Chile. Paula Escobar", *https://www.youtube.com/watch?reload=9&v=TFQniQmDTpk*, https://www.youtube.com/watch?reload=9&v=TFQniQmDTpk (accessed on 25 January 2021). [1]

Fernandez, J. and K. Lopez (2020), *Radiografía a la violencia intrafamiliar en pandemia: la deuda del Estado*, https://www.theclinic.cl/2020/08/17/radiografia-a-la-violencia-intrafamiliar-en (accessed on 25 January 2021).   [20]

Gandara, F. (2020), *Violence Against Women in Chile Intensifies During Pandemic*, https://chiletoday.cl/violence-against-women-in-chile-intensifies-during-pandemic/.   [21]

Gutierrez, D., G. Martin and H. Nopo (2020), *The coronavirus pandemic and its challenges to women's work in Latin America*, http://www.grade.org.pe/en/publicaciones/the-coronavirus-pandemic-and-its-challenges-to-womens-work-in-latin-america/ (accessed on 25 January 2021).   [6]

INE (2020), *Banco de datos de la Encuesta Nacional de Empleo*, http://bancodatosene.ine.cl/.   [4]

INE (2020), *Boletín estadístico: Empleo trimestral*, Instituto Nacinal de Estadísticas, Santiago, https://www.ine.cl/docs/default-source/ocupacion-y-desocupacion/boletines/2020/pa%C3%ADs/bolet%C3%ADn-empleo-nacional-trimestre-m%C3%B3vil-marzo-abril-mayo-2020.pdf?sfvrsn=bf85a27_6.   [3]

Infoseguras (2020), *#MujeresSeguras – Campaña Regional de prevención de violencia contra las mujeres*, https://infosegura.org/2020/09/24/mujeresseguras-campana-regional-de-prevencion-de-violencia-contra-las-mujeres/ (accessed on 25 January 2021).   [19]

MINEDUC (2020), *Apoyos del Mineduc durante la pandemia del Covid-19*, https://www.mineduc.cl/aprendo-en-linea-docente/ (accessed on 2 July 2020).   [8]

Ministerio de Desarrollo Social (2017), *ADULTOS MAYORES Síntesis de resultados Contenidos*, http://www.desarrollosocial.cl (accessed on 18 February 2021).   [11]

MinMujEG (2021), *Encuesta de Evaluación Rápida sobre el Impacto del COVID-19*, https://minmujeryeg.gob.cl/wp-content/uploads/2020/11/Resutados-RGA-Chile_Final-Web.pdf (accessed on 23 March 2020).   [12]

MINMUJERyEG (2020), "Ministra Santelices se reúne con Carabineros para abordar aumento de llamadas por violencia", *Ministerio de la Mujer y la Equidad de Género*, https://minmujeryeg.gob.cl/?p=40152 (accessed on 2 January 2020).   [22]

OEA (2020), *COVID-19 en la vida de las mujeres: Razones para reconocer los impactos diferenciados*, https://iris.paho.org/bitstream/handle/10665.2/52034/OPSNMHMHCovid19200008_spa.pdf.   [15]

OECD (2020), *OECD Economic Outlook*, OECD Publishing, Paris, https://doi.org/10.1787/34bfd999-en.   [2]

OECD (2020), "Women at the core of the fight against COVID-19 crisis", *OECD Policy Responses to Coronavirus (COVID-19)*, OECD Publishing, Paris, https://doi.org/10.1787/553a8269-en.   [24]

PAHO (2020), *COVID-19 y la violencia contra la mujer: Lo que el sector y el sistema de salud pueden hacer*, https://iris.paho.org/bitstream/handle/10665.2/52034/OPSNMHMHCovid19200008_spa.pdf.   [16]

UN WOMEN (2020), *Prevencion de la violencia de las mujeres frente a COVID-19*, [17]
https://www2.unwomen.org/-/media/field%20office%20americas/documentos/publicaciones/2020/05/es_prevencion%20de%20violencia%20contra%20las%20mujeresbrief%20espanol.pdf?la=es&vs=3033.

UNDP (2020), *No Safer Place than Home? The Increase in Domestic and Gender-based Violence During COVID-19 Lockdowns in LAC*, [18]
https://www.latinamerica.undp.org/content/rblac/en/home/presscenter/director-s-graph-for-thought/no-safer-place-than-home---the-increase-in-domestic-and-gender-b.html (accessed on 25 January 2021).

UNICEF (2020), *The impact of COVID-19 on the mental health of adolescents and youth*, [14]
https://www.unicef.org/lac/en/impact-covid-19-mental-health-adolescents-and-youth (accessed on 25 January 2021).

University of Chile and IMIIMPP (2020), *Modos de sentir: experiencia de vida cotidiana en pandemia*, https://www.uchile.cl/documentos/vida-en-pandemia-informe-1b-experiencia-frente-a-la-crisis_166860_1_2718.pdf (accessed on 25 January 2021). [13]

Women, UN; ECLAC; (2020), *Care in Latin America and the Caribbean during the COVID-19: Towards comprehensive systems to strengthen response and recovery*, [7]
https://www.cepal.org/en/publications/45917-care-latin-america-and-caribbean-during-covid-19-towards-comprehensive-systems (accessed on 25 January 2021).

Notes

[1] Chilean Chamber of Deputies (2020), *Proyecto de ley que establece normas para el retorno seguro en la educación inicial, en el contexto de la pandemia COVID-19*, https://www.camara.cl/verDoc.aspx?prmID=14044&prmTIPO=INICIATIVA.

www.ingramcontent.com/pod-product-compliance
Lightning Source LLC
Chambersburg PA
CBHW081511200326
41518CB00015B/2462